# salads
## *for summer*

# salads
## *for summer*

### creative salads to delight and inspire

Love Food ® is an imprint of Parragon Books Ltd

Parragon
Queen Street House
4 Queen Street
Bath BA1 1HE, UK

ISBN: 978-1-4075-5441-9

Printed in China

Photography by Günter Beer
Home Economy by Stevan Paul
Internal Design by Talking Design
Introduction and additional recipes written by
Beverly Le Blanc

NOTES FOR THE READER

This book uses both metric and imperial
measurements. Follow the same units of
measurement throughout; do not mix metric
and imperial. All spoon measurements are
level: teaspoons are assumed to be 5 ml, and
tablespoons are assumed to be 15 ml. Unless
otherwise stated, milk is assumed to be full fat,
eggs and individual vegetables are medium,
and pepper is freshly ground black pepper.

The times given are an approximate guide
only. Preparation times differ according to the
techniques used by different people and the
cooking times may also vary from those given.
Optional ingredients, variations or serving
suggestions have not been included in the
calculations.

Recipes using raw or very lightly cooked
eggs should be avoided by infants, the
elderly, pregnant women, convalescents and
anyone suffering from an illness. Pregnant and
breastfeeding women are advised to avoid eating
peanuts and peanut products. Sufferers from
nut allergies should be aware that some of the
ready-made ingredients used in the recipes in
this book may contain nuts. Always check the
packaging before use.

# contents

# The taste of summer all year round

Take a fresh look at salads and you'll see there are a lot of exciting developments in the salad bowl. Banished forever is the image of salads as dull diet food consisting of little more than limp lettuce and soggy, flavourless tomatoes.

Today, salads are among the ultimate health foods. They can contain an exciting variety of colourful, delicious and satisfying ingredients that provide the nutrients essential for healthy living. You'll find plenty of inspiration in this book for a cornucopia of healthy salads for all occasions, from light lunches and family meals to stylish dinner parties. And, remember, salads aren't just for summer. We have plenty of ideas for salads that brighten and lighten winter mealtimes, too. In fact, once you get into the habit of thinking 'salad' while menu planning, ideas will also come to you whatever the time of the year as you push your trolley along the supermarket aisles or stop at the cheese counter or produce department.

Salads are versatile enough to cater for vegetarians and meat-eaters alike. Meat, seafood and poultry are ideal salad ingredients, along with the perhaps more commonly used lettuce and other leaves, vegetables, fruit, herbs, nuts, seeds, grains, pulses and cheese. And with so many ingredients to choose from, salads can be as simple and light or complex and filling as you like. They also have an added bonus in that they are versatile enough to fit easily into all your meal plans, from starters through to desserts.

As you flip through these recipes you'll find classic favourites – Caesar Salad, Chef's Salad and Salad Niçoise, to name a few – as well as fresh, new ideas that capture the flavours of cuisines around the world. If, for example, the idea of chicken salad doesn't excite because you've been making the same recipe out of habit for as long as you can remember, try Thai-style Chicken Salad (page 102). You'll never think of chicken salad as humdrum again!

## Bowls of Goodness

It wasn't long ago that when 'salads' and 'health' were linked it was in the context of weight-reducing diets that were restrictive and ultimately unsatisfying. Today, however, salads are a delicious component of a healthy diet, giving you endless variety at mealtimes without long hours in the kitchen.

With fresh produce from all corners of the globe readily available in supermarkets and gourmet food shops, you can enjoy a variety of salads all year round but, remember, salads are at their most flavoursome and nutritious when made with seasonal produce in its prime.

We are all being urged to eat more fruit and vegetables every day, and a salad a day can

go a long way to help you meet the minimum target of five portions. Enjoy a bowl of Traditional Greek Salad (page 17) or Three-Colour Salad (page 34), for example, and you'll be more than halfway to success. What could be easier – or more enjoyable?

Salads also make great accompaniments, served alongside a filling bowl of pasta or a plate of hot or cold roast meat.

So, if you regularly fall back on the old favourite of just tossing a few green leaves with a simple oil-and-vinegar dressing, it's definitely time to think again. It's very easy to mix and match ingredients and the choice has never been greater. And don't make the mistake of thinking all salad ingredients have to be raw, either. Adding small amounts of cooked meat, poultry and seafood to lettuce leaves and other vegetables gives you a satisfying meal. If you want a meal-in-a-bowl, try Roast Pork & Pumpkin Salad (page 113), Smoked Chicken Salad with Avocado & Tarragon Dressing (page 110) and Prawn & Rice Salad (page 145), for example. There are plenty of vegetarian main-course salads, too, such as the Middle Eastern favourite Tabbouleh (see page 190) and Buckwheat Noodle Salad with Smoked Tofu (page 193).

Cooked vegetables also make good salad ingredients. Grilled peppers, fried aubergines, blanched beans of all varieties and peas are just some of the cooked veggies you'll find adding flavour and an extra dimension to the salads in this book.

## Colourful Greens

Even with so many ingredients to choose from, salad greens still provide the backbone of many popular salads. Take a look around your supermarket or greengrocer's and you'll see leaves in many colours and textures, ranging from pearly, pale white chicory to bright red and white radicchio. They also have a variety of flavours, from robust and peppery to sweet, nutty and mild.

The greater the variety of leaves you include in your salad, the more interesting it will be, and the more nutrients it will contain. When you select salad leaves, remember that the darker coloured ones, such as spinach leaves, contain more beta-carotene, which helps fight some forms of cancer and other illnesses. Leafy green vegetables are also excellent sources of fibre.

It's become very convenient to grab a bag of mixed salad leaves at the supermarket, but it can be more satisfying to sample a selection of greens sold separately at greengrocers and farmers' markets. Asian and other ethnic food shops are also a good source of unusual greens.

Try these new and familiar greens to add variety to your salad bowl:

• Beet greens – distinctive with their ruby-red stalks, these soft leaves are mildly flavoured.

• Cos lettuce – Caesar Salad (page 14) simply wouldn't be Caesar Salad without these long, crisp leaves. Comes in a large, compact head with long, crisp leaves that have a sweet nutty flavour.

• Lamb's lettuce – also labelled as corn salad or mâche, these tender leaves have a mild, slightly nutty flavour.

• Mesclun or mesclum – now sold in supermarkets,

this French mix of leaves can include chervil, dandelion, oakleaf lettuce and rocket, along with other leaves. Just add dressing and toss.

• Mizuna – from the Far East, this winter green has a full peppery flavour. Its pointy green leaves add visual interest to salads, too.

• Nasturtium – use both the colourful flowers and peppery leaves in salads.

• Radicchio – there is nothing like the bright red and white leaves of this member of the bitter chicory family to liven autumn and early winter salads. It has a crisp texture and nutty, peppery flavour.

• Red chard – like beet greens, these fibre-rich leaves have bright red stalks and sometimes the leaves are tinged red as well.

• Rocket – known for their pronounced peppery flavour, these dark green leaves perk up many salads. Popular in Italian salads. Substitute watercress if you can't find rocket.

## Keep It Fresh

Good salads are only made with good ingredients, and freshness is all-important when buying salad greens. Because of the leaves' high water content, they are very perishable, so buy them as close as possible to serving. Not only will they taste best, they will also contain the most nutrients when they are in peak condition.

Let your eyes guide you when you are shopping for salad leaves — fresh leaves look fresh. They aren't tinged with brown, nor are they wilted or slimy.

When you get salad ingredients home, give them a rinse in cold water, then spin them dry or use a tea towel to pat them dry. Never leave them to soak in a sink of cold water because all the water-soluble vitamins and minerals will escape.

Use leafy ingredients as soon as possible, but most will keep for up to four days in a sealed container in the fridge. Once you open bags of prepared leaves, however, they should be used within 24 hours. You can prepare salad greens several hours in advance and store in the fridge, but do not dress until just before serving, because the acid in most dressings causes the leaves to wilt and become unappetizing.

# sunshine
a collection of vegetable salads

# caesar salad

**serves 4**

**ingredients**

1 large egg

2 cos lettuces or 3 Little Gem lettuces

6 tbsp olive oil

2 tbsp lemon juice

salt and pepper

8 canned anchovy fillets, drained and
    roughly chopped

85 g/3 oz fresh Parmesan cheese shavings

**garlic croûtons**

4 tbsp olive oil

2 garlic cloves

5 slices white bread, crusts removed,
    cut into 1-cm/$\frac{1}{2}$-inch cubes

Bring a small, heavy-based saucepan of water to the boil.

Meanwhile, make the garlic croûtons. Heat the olive oil in a heavy-based frying pan. Add the garlic and diced bread and cook, stirring and tossing frequently, for 4–5 minutes, or until the bread is crispy and golden all over. Remove from the frying pan with a slotted spoon and drain on kitchen paper.

While the bread is frying, add the egg to the boiling water and cook for 1 minute, then remove from the saucepan and reserve.

Arrange the lettuce leaves in a salad bowl. Mix the olive oil and lemon juice together, then season to taste with salt and pepper. Crack the egg into the dressing and whisk to blend. Pour the dressing over the lettuce leaves, toss well, then add the croûtons and chopped anchovies and toss the salad again. Sprinkle with Parmesan cheese shavings and serve.

# traditional greek salad

serves 4

**ingredients**

200 g/7 oz Greek feta cheese

$\frac{1}{2}$ head of iceberg lettuce or 1 lettuce such
  as cos or escarole, shredded or sliced

4 tomatoes, quartered

$\frac{1}{2}$ cucumber, sliced

12 Greek black olives, stoned

2 tbsp chopped fresh herbs such as
  oregano, flat-leaf parsley, mint or basil

**for the dressing**

6 tbsp extra-virgin olive oil

2 tbsp fresh lemon juice

1 garlic clove, crushed

pinch of sugar

salt and pepper

Make the dressing by whisking together the oil, lemon juice, garlic, sugar, salt and pepper in a small bowl. Set aside. Cut the feta cheese into cubes about 2.5 cm/1 inch square. Put the lettuce, tomatoes and cucumber in a salad bowl. Scatter over the cheese and toss together.

Just before serving, whisk the dressing, pour over the salad leaves and toss together. Scatter over the olives and chopped herbs and serve.

# mozzarella salad with sun-dried tomatoes

serves 4

**ingredients**

100 g/3½ oz mixed salad leaves, such
    as oakleaf lettuce, baby spinach and
    rocket

500 g/1 lb 2 oz smoked mozzarella, sliced

**for the dressing**

140 g/5 oz sun-dried tomatoes in olive oil
    (drained weight), reserving the oil from
    the bottle

15 g/½ oz fresh basil, coarsely shredded

15 g/½ oz fresh flat-leaf parsley,
    coarsely chopped

1 tbsp capers, rinsed

1 tbsp balsamic vinegar

1 garlic clove, coarsely chopped

extra olive oil, if necessary

pepper

Put the sun-dried tomatoes, basil, parsley, capers, vinegar and garlic in a food processor or blender. Measure the oil from the sun-dried tomatoes jar and make it up to 150 ml/5 fl oz with more olive oil if necessary. Add it to the food processor or blender and process until smooth. Season to taste with pepper.

Divide the salad leaves between 4 individual serving plates. Top with the slices of mozzarella and spoon the dressing over them. Serve immediately.

# red & green salad

serves 4

**ingredients**

650 g/1 lb 7 oz cooked beetroot

3 tbsp extra-virgin olive oil

juice of 1 orange

1 tsp caster sugar

1 tsp fennel seeds

salt and pepper

115 g/4 oz fresh baby spinach leaves

Using a sharp knife, dice the cooked beetroot and reserve until required. Heat the olive oil in a small, heavy-based saucepan. Add the orange juice, sugar and fennel seeds and season to taste with salt and pepper. Stir constantly until the sugar has dissolved.

Add the reserved beetroot to the saucepan and stir gently to coat. Remove the saucepan from the heat.

Arrange the baby spinach leaves in a large salad bowl. Spoon the warmed beetroot on top and serve immediately.

# roasted garlic, sweet potato, grilled aubergine & pepper salad with mozzarella

serves 4

**ingredients**

2 sweet potatoes, peeled and cut into
    chunks
2 tbsp olive oil
pepper
2 garlic cloves, crushed
1 large aubergine, sliced
2 red peppers, deseeded and sliced
200 g/7 oz mixed salad leaves
2 x 150 g/5½ oz mozzarella cheeses,
    drained and sliced

**for the dressing**

1 tbsp balsamic vinegar
1 garlic clove, crushed
3 tbsp olive oil
1 small shallot, finely chopped
2 tbsp chopped mixed fresh herbs,
    such as tarragon, chervil and basil
pepper

Preheat the oven to 190°C/375°F/Gas Mark 5. Put the sweet potato chunks into a roasting tin with the oil, pepper to taste and garlic and toss to combine. Roast in the preheated oven for 30 minutes, or until soft and slightly charred.

Meanwhile, preheat the grill to high. Arrange the aubergine and pepper slices on the grill pan and cook under the preheated grill, turning occasionally, for 10 minutes, or until soft and slightly charred.

To make the dressing, whisk the vinegar, garlic and oil together in a small bowl and stir in the shallot and herbs. Season to taste with pepper.

To serve, divide the salad leaves between 4 serving plates and arrange the sweet potato, aubergine, peppers and mozzarella on top. Drizzle with the dressing and serve.

# mixed mushroom salad

**serves 4**

**ingredients**

3 tbsp pine kernels

2 red onions, cut into chunks

4 tbsp olive oil

2 garlic cloves, crushed

3 slices Granary bread, cubed

200 g/7 oz mixed salad leaves

250 g/9 oz chestnut mushrooms, sliced

150 g/5½ oz shiitake mushrooms, sliced

150 g/5½ oz oyster mushrooms, torn

**for the dressing**

1 garlic clove, crushed

2 tbsp red wine vinegar

4 tbsp walnut oil

1 tbsp finely chopped fresh parsley

pepper

Preheat the oven to 180°C/350°F/Gas Mark 4. Heat a non-stick frying pan over a medium heat, add the pine kernels and cook, turning, until just browned. Tip into a bowl and set aside.

Put the onions and 1 tablespoon of the olive oil into a roasting tin and toss to coat. Roast in the preheated oven for 30 minutes.

Meanwhile, heat 1 tablespoon of the remaining oil with the garlic in the non-stick frying pan over a high heat. Add the bread and cook, turning frequently, for 5 minutes, or until brown and crisp. Remove from the pan and set aside.

Divide the salad leaves between 4 serving plates and add the roasted onions. To make the dressing, whisk the garlic, vinegar and oil together in a small bowl. Stir in the parsley and season to taste with pepper. Drizzle over the salad and onions.

Heat the remaining oil in a frying pan, add the chestnut and shiitake mushrooms and cook for 2–3 minutes, stirring frequently. Add the oyster mushrooms and cook for a further 2–3 minutes. Divide the hot mushroom mixture between the 4 plates. Scatter over the pine kernels and croûtons and serve.

# warm red lentil salad with goat's cheese

serves 4

**ingredients**

2 tbsp olive oil

2 tsp cumin seeds

2 garlic cloves, crushed

2 tsp grated fresh root ginger

300 g/10½ oz split red lentils

700 ml/1¼ pints vegetable stock

2 tbsp chopped fresh mint

2 tbsp chopped fresh coriander

2 red onions, thinly sliced

200 g/7 oz baby spinach leaves

1 tsp hazelnut oil

150 g/5½ oz soft goat's cheese

4 tbsp Greek yogurt

pepper

Heat half the olive oil in a large saucepan over a medium heat, add the cumin seeds, garlic and ginger and cook for 2 minutes, stirring constantly.

Stir in the lentils, then add the stock, a ladleful at a time, until it is all absorbed, stirring constantly – this will take about 20 minutes. Remove from the heat and stir in the herbs.

Meanwhile, heat the remaining olive oil in a frying pan over a medium heat, add the onions and cook, stirring frequently, for 10 minutes, or until soft and lightly browned.

Toss the spinach in the hazelnut oil in a bowl, then divide between 4 serving plates.

Mash the goat's cheese with the yogurt in a small bowl and season to taste with pepper.

Divide the lentils between the serving plates and top with the onions and goat's cheese mixture.

# green bean & walnut salad

**ingredients**

450 g/1 lb green beans

1 small onion, finely chopped

1 garlic clove, chopped

4 tbsp freshly grated Parmesan cheese

2 tbsp chopped walnuts or almonds,
    to garnish

**for the dressing**

6 tbsp olive oil

2 tbsp white wine vinegar

salt and pepper

2 tsp chopped fresh tarragon

Top and tail the beans, but leave them whole. Cook for
3–4 minutes in salted boiling water. Drain well, run under the
cold tap to refresh and drain again. Put into a mixing bowl and
add the onion, garlic and cheese.

Place the dressing ingredients in a jar with a screw-top lid. Shake
well. Pour the dressing over the salad and toss gently to coat.
Cover with clingfilm and chill for at least 30 minutes. Remove the
beans from the refrigerator 10 minutes before serving. Give them
a quick stir and transfer to attractive serving dishes.

Toast the nuts in a dry frying pan over a medium heat for
2 minutes, or until they begin to brown. Sprinkle the toasted
nuts over the beans to garnish before serving.

# red onion, tomato & herb salad

**serves 4**

**ingredients**

900 g/2 lb tomatoes, sliced thinly

1 tbsp sugar (optional)

salt and pepper

1 red onion, sliced thinly into rings

large handful coarsely chopped fresh herbs

**for the dressing**

2–4 tbsp vegetable oil

2 tbsp red wine vinegar or fruit vinegar

Arrange the tomato slices in a shallow bowl. Sprinkle with sugar (if using), and salt and pepper.

Separate the onion slices into rings and scatter over the tomatoes. Sprinkle the herbs over the top. Anything that is in season can be used – for example, tarragon, sorrel, coriander or basil.

Place the dressing ingredients in a jar with a screw-top lid. Shake well. Pour the dressing over the salad and mix gently. Cover with clingfilm and refrigerate for 20 minutes. Remove the salad from the refrigerator 5 minutes before serving.

# nutty beetroot salad

serves 4

ingredients

3 tbsp red wine vinegar or fruit vinegar

3 cooked beetroot, grated

2 tart apples, such as Granny Smith

2 tbsp lemon juice

4 large handfuls mixed salad leaves,
    to serve

4 tbsp pecans, to garnish

for the dressing

50 ml/2 fl oz plain yogurt

50 ml/2 fl oz mayonnaise

1 garlic clove, chopped

1 tbsp chopped fresh dill

salt and pepper

Sprinkle vinegar over the beetroot, cover with clingfilm and chill for at least 4 hours.

Core and slice the apples, place the slices in a dish and sprinkle with the lemon juice to prevent discoloration.

Combine the dressing ingredients in a small bowl. Remove the beetroot from the refrigerator and dress. Add the apples to the beetroot and mix gently to coat with the salad dressing.

To serve, arrange a handful of salad leaves on each plate and top with a large spoonful of the apple and beetroot mixture.

Toast the pecans in a dry frying pan over a medium heat for 2 minutes, or until they begin to brown. Sprinkle over the beetroot and apple to garnish.

# three-colour salad

serves 4

**ingredients**
280 g/10 oz buffalo mozzarella, drained
   and thinly sliced
8 beef tomatoes, sliced
salt and pepper
20 fresh basil leaves
125 ml/4 fl oz extra-virgin olive oil

Arrange the mozzarella and tomato slices on 4 individual serving plates and season to taste with salt. Set aside in a cool place for 30 minutes.

Sprinkle the basil leaves over the salad and drizzle with the olive oil. Season with pepper and serve immediately.

# grilled pepper salad

serves 4 – 6

**ingredients**
6 large red, orange or yellow peppers,
    each cut in half lengthways, grilled
    and peeled
4 hard-boiled eggs, shelled
12 anchovy fillets in oil, drained
12 large black olives, stoned
extra-virgin olive oil or garlic-flavoured
    olive oil, for drizzling
sherry vinegar, to taste
salt and pepper
crusty bread, to serve

Remove any cores and seeds from the grilled peppers and cut into thin strips. Arrange on a serving platter.

Cut the eggs into wedges and arrange over the pepper strips, along with the anchovy fillets and olives.

Drizzle oil over the top, then splash with sherry vinegar, adding both to taste. Sprinkle a little salt and pepper over the top and serve with bread.

# tomato salad with fried feta

**serves 4**

**ingredients**

12 plum tomatoes, sliced

1 very small red onion, thinly sliced

15 g/½ oz rocket leaves

20 Greek black olives, stoned

200 g/7 oz Greek feta cheese

1 egg

3 tbsp plain white flour

2 tbsp olive oil

**for the dressing**

3 tbsp extra-virgin olive oil

juice of ½ lemon

2 tsp chopped fresh oregano

pinch of sugar

pepper

Make the dressing by whisking together the extra virgin olive oil, the lemon juice, oregano, sugar and pepper in a small bowl. Set aside.

Prepare the salad by arranging the tomatoes, onion, rocket and olives on 4 individual plates.

Cut the feta cheese into cubes about 2.5 cm/1 inch square. Beat the egg in a dish and put the flour on a separate plate. Coat the cheese in the egg, shake off the excess, and then coat in the flour.

Heat the olive oil in a large frying pan, add the cheese and fry over a medium heat, turning over the cubes of cheese until they are golden on all sides.

Scatter the fried feta over the salad. Whisk together the prepared dressing, spoon over the salad and serve warm.

# grilled pepper salad with goat's cheese

**serves 4**

**ingredients**

2 red peppers

2 green peppers

2 yellow or orange peppers

125 ml/4 fl oz vinaigrette or
herb vinaigrette

6 spring onions, finely chopped

1 tbsp capers in brine, rinsed

200 g/7 oz soft goat's cheese,
any rind removed

chopped fresh flat-leaf parsley, to serve

Preheat the grill to high. Arrange the peppers on a grill pan, position about 10 cm/4 inches from the heat and grill for 8–10 minutes, turning them frequently, until the skins are charred all over. Transfer the peppers to a bowl, cover with a damp tea towel and leave to stand until cool enough to handle.

Using a small knife, peel each of the peppers. Working over a bowl to catch the juices from inside the peppers, cut each pepper in half and remove the cores and seeds, then cut the flesh into thin strips.

Arrange the peppers on a serving platter and spoon over the reserved juices, then add the dressing. Sprinkle over the spring onions and capers, then crumble over the cheese. If not serving immediately, cover and chill until required. Sprinkle with the parsley to serve.

# broad bean salad

**serves 4**

**ingredients**

1.3 kg/3 lb fresh young broad beans or
    675 g/1½ lb frozen baby broad beans
150 g/5½ oz Greek feta cheese
1 bunch spring onions, thinly sliced
2 tbsp chopped fresh dill or mint
2 hard-boiled eggs, quartered
crusty bread
greek yogurt, to serve (optional)

**for the dressing**

6 tbsp extra-virgin olive oil
grated rind of 1 lemon and
    2 tbsp lemon juice
1 small garlic clove, crushed
pinch of sugar
pepper

Make the dressing by whisking together the oil, lemon rind and juice, garlic, sugar and pepper in a small bowl. Set aside. Shell the fresh broad beans, if using, and cook in boiling salted water for 5–10 minutes, or until tender. If using frozen broad beans, cook in boiling salted water for 4–5 minutes. Drain the cooked beans and put in a salad bowl.

Whisk the dressing and pour over the beans while they are still warm. Crumble over the feta cheese, add the spring onions and toss together. Sprinkle over the chopped dill and arrange the egg quarters in the bowl.

Serve warm with crusty bread and a bowl of yogurt to spoon on top, if wished.

# mexican tomato salad

**serves 4**

**ingredients**

600 g/1 lb 5 oz tomatoes, peeled,
  deseeded and roughly chopped
1 onion, thinly sliced and pushed
  out into rings
400 g/14 oz canned kidney beans,
  drained and rinsed

**for the dressing**

1 fresh green chilli, deseeded and diced
3 tbsp chopped fresh coriander
3 tbsp olive oil
1 garlic clove, finely chopped
4 tbsp lime juice
salt and pepper

Place the chopped tomatoes and onion slices in a large serving bowl and mix well. Stir in the kidney beans.

Mix the chilli, coriander, olive oil, garlic and lime juice together in a jug and season to taste with salt and pepper.

Pour the dressing over the salad and toss thoroughly. Serve immediately or cover with clingfilm and leave to chill in the refrigerator until required.

# thai noodle salad

**ingredients**

25 g/1 oz dried wood ears
55 g/2 oz dried Chinese mushrooms
115 g/4 oz cellophane noodles
115 g/4 oz cooked lean minced pork
115 g/4 oz peeled raw prawns
5 fresh red chillies, deseeded and
    thinly sliced
1 tbsp chopped fresh coriander
3 tbsp Thai fish sauce
3 tbsp lime juice
1 tbsp brown sugar

Put the wood ears and Chinese mushrooms in separate bowls and pour over enough boiling water to cover. Leave to soak for 30 minutes. After 20 minutes, put the cellophane noodles in a separate bowl and pour over enough hot water to cover. Leave the noodles to soak for 10 minutes, or according to the packet instructions.

Drain the wood ears, rinse thoroughly and cut into small pieces. Drain the mushrooms, squeezing out as much liquid as possible. Cut off and discard the stalks and cut the caps in half. Pour just enough water into a saucepan to cover the base and bring to the boil. Add the pork, prawns, wood ears and mushrooms and simmer, stirring, for 3 minutes, or until the prawns are cooked through. Drain well. Drain the noodles and cut them into short lengths with kitchen scissors.

Place the chillies, coriander, fish sauce, lime juice and brown sugar in a salad bowl and stir until the sugar has dissolved. Add the noodles and the prawn and pork mixture, toss well and serve.

# sweet potato & bean salad

serves 4

**ingredients**

1 sweet potato
4 baby carrots, halved
4 tomatoes
4 celery sticks, chopped
225 g/8 oz canned borlotti beans,
    drained and rinsed
115 g/4 oz mixed salad leaves,
    such as frisée, rocket, radicchio
    and oakleaf lettuce
1 tbsp sultanas
4 spring onions, sliced diagonally

**for the dressing**

2 tbsp lemon juice
1 garlic clove, crushed
150 ml/5 fl oz natural yogurt
2 tbsp olive oil
salt and pepper

Peel and dice the sweet potato. Bring a saucepan of water to the boil over a medium heat. Add the sweet potato and cook for 10 minutes, or until tender. Drain, transfer to a bowl and reserve until required.

Cook the carrots in a separate saucepan of boiling water for 1 minute. Drain thoroughly and add to the sweet potato. Cut the tops off the tomatoes and scoop out the seeds. Chop the flesh and add to the bowl with the celery and beans. Mix well.

Line a large serving bowl with the mixed salad leaves. Spoon the sweet potato and bean mixture on top, then sprinkle with the sultanas and spring onions.

Put all the dressing ingredients in a screw-top jar, with salt and pepper to taste, screw on the lid and shake until well blended. Pour over the salad and serve.

# raspberry & feta salad with couscous

**serves 6**

**ingredients**

350 g/12 oz couscous
600 ml/1 pint boiling chicken stock or
    vegetable stock
350 g/12 oz fresh raspberries
small bunch of fresh basil
225 g/8 oz feta cheese, cubed or crumbled
2 courgettes, thinly sliced
4 spring onions, trimmed and
    diagonally sliced
55 g/2 oz pine kernels, toasted
grated rind of 1 lemon

**for the dressing**

1 tbsp white wine vinegar
1 tbsp balsamic vinegar
4 tbsp extra-virgin olive oil
juice of 1 lemon
salt and pepper

Put the couscous in a large, heatproof bowl and pour over the stock. Stir well, cover and leave to soak until all the stock has been absorbed.

Pick over the raspberries, discarding any that are overripe. Shred the basil leaves.

Transfer the couscous to a large serving bowl and stir well to break up any lumps. Add the cheese, courgettes, spring onions, raspberries and pine kernels. Stir in the basil and lemon rind and gently toss all the ingredients together.

Put all the dressing ingredients in a screw-top jar, with salt and pepper to taste, screw on the lid and shake until well blended. Pour over the salad and serve.

# orecchiette salad with pears & stilton

**serves 4**

**ingredients**

250 g/9 oz dried orecchiette

1 head radicchio, torn into pieces

1 oakleaf lettuce, torn into pieces

2 pears

1 tbsp lemon juice

250 g/9 oz Stilton cheese, diced

55 g/2 oz chopped walnuts

4 tomatoes, quartered

1 red onion, sliced

1 carrot, grated

8 fresh basil leaves

55 g/2 oz lamb's lettuce

**for the dressing**

4 tbsp olive oil

2 tbsp lemon juice

salt and pepper

Bring a large, heavy-based saucepan of lightly salted water to the boil. Add the pasta, return to the boil and cook for 8–10 minutes, or until tender but still firm to the bite. Drain, refresh in a bowl of cold water and drain again.

Place the radicchio and oakleaf lettuce leaves in a salad bowl. Halve the pears, remove the cores and dice the flesh. Toss the diced pear with 1 tablespoon of lemon juice in a small bowl to prevent discoloration. Top the salad with the Stilton, walnuts, pears, pasta, tomatoes, onion slices and grated carrot. Add the basil and lamb's lettuce.

For the dressing, mix the lemon juice and the olive oil and vinegar together in a jug, then season to taste with salt and pepper. Pour the dressing over the salad, toss and serve.

# salad with garlic dressing

serves 4

**ingredients**

85 g/3 oz cucumber, cut into batons

6 spring onions, halved

2 tomatoes, deseeded and
   cut into 8 wedges

1 yellow pepper, deseeded and
   cut into strips

2 celery sticks, cut into strips

4 radishes, quartered

85 g/3 oz rocket

1 tbsp chopped fresh mint,
   to garnish (optional)

**for the dressing**

2 tbsp lemon juice

1 garlic clove, crushed

150 ml/5 fl oz natural yogurt

2 tbsp olive oil

salt and pepper

To make the salad, gently mix the cucumber batons, spring onions, tomato wedges, yellow pepper strips, celery, radishes and rocket in a large serving bowl.

To make the dressing, stir the lemon juice, garlic, natural yogurt and olive oil together in a small bowl until thoroughly combined. Season with salt and pepper to taste.

Spoon the dressing over the salad and toss to mix. Sprinkle the salad with chopped mint (if using) and serve.

# warm pasta salad

serves 4

**ingredients**

225 g/8 oz dried farfalle or
   other pasta shapes
6 pieces of sun-dried tomato in oil,
   drained and chopped
4 spring onions, chopped
55 g/2 oz rocket, shredded
1/2 cucumber, deseeded and diced
salt and pepper

**for the dressing**

4 tbsp olive oil
1 tbsp white wine vinegar
1/2 tsp caster sugar
1 tsp Dijon mustard
salt and pepper
4 fresh basil leaves, finely shredded

To make the dressing, whisk the olive oil, vinegar, sugar and mustard together in a jug. Season to taste with salt and pepper and stir in the basil.

Bring a large, heavy-based saucepan of lightly salted water to the boil. Add the pasta, return to the boil and cook for 8–10 minutes, or until tender but still firm to the bite. Drain and transfer to a salad bowl. Add the dressing and toss well.

Add the tomatoes, spring onions, rocket and cucumber, season to taste with salt and pepper and toss. Serve warm.

# italian salad

**ingredients**

225 g/8 oz dried conchiglie (pasta shells)

50 g/1¾ oz pine kernels

350 g/12 oz cherry tomatoes, halved

1 red pepper, deseeded and cut into
  bite-sized chunks

1 red onion, chopped

200 g/7 oz buffalo mozzarella, cut into
  small pieces

12 black olives, stoned

25 g/1 oz fresh basil leaves

shavings of fresh Parmesan cheese,
  to garnish

crusty bread, to serve

**for the dressing**

5 tbsp extra-virgin olive oil

2 tbsp balsamic vinegar

1 tbsp chopped fresh basil

salt and pepper

Bring a large saucepan of lightly salted water to the boil. Add the pasta and cook over a medium heat for about 10 minutes, or according to the packet instructions. When cooked, the pasta should be tender but still firm to the bite. Drain, rinse under cold running water and drain again. Leave to cool.

While the pasta is cooking, put the pine kernels in a dry frying pan and cook over a low heat for 1–2 minutes until golden brown. Remove from the heat, transfer to a dish and leave to cool.

To make the dressing, put the oil, vinegar and basil into a small bowl. Season with salt and pepper and stir together well. Cover with clingfilm and set to one side.

To assemble the salad, divide the pasta between serving bowls. Add the pine kernels, tomatoes, red pepper, onion, cheese and olives. Scatter over the basil leaves, then drizzle over the dressing. Garnish with fresh Parmesan cheese shavings and serve with crusty bread.

# potato salad

serves 4

**ingredients**

700 g/1 lb 9 oz new potatoes

8 spring onions

250 ml/9 fl oz mayonnaise

1 tsp paprika

salt and pepper

2 tbsp snipped fresh chives

pinch of paprika, to garnish

Bring a large saucepan of lightly salted water to the boil. Add the potatoes and cook for 10–15 minutes, or until they are just tender.

Drain the potatoes and rinse them under cold running water until completely cold. Drain again. Transfer the potatoes to a bowl and reserve until required.

Using a sharp knife, slice the spring onions thinly on the diagonal.

Mix the mayonnaise, paprika and salt and pepper to taste together in a bowl. Pour the mixture over the potatoes. Add the spring onions to the potatoes and toss together.

Transfer the potato salad to a serving bowl, and sprinkle with snipped chives and a pinch of paprika. Cover and leave to chill in the refrigerator until required.

# capri salad

serves 4

**ingredients**

2 beef tomatoes

125 g/4½ oz mozzarella cheese

12 black olives

8 fresh basil leaves

1 tbsp balsamic vinegar

1 tbsp extra-virgin olive oil

salt and pepper

fresh basil leaves, to garnish

Using a sharp knife, cut the tomatoes into thin slices. Drain the mozzarella, if necessary, and cut into slices and stone the black olives before slicing into rings.

Layer the tomatoes, mozzarella slices, olives and basil leaves in 4 stacks, finishing with a layer of cheese on top.

Place each stack under a preheated hot grill for 2–3 minutes or just long enough to melt the mozzarella.

Drizzle over the balsamic vinegar and olive oil, and season to taste with a little salt and pepper.

Transfer to individual serving plates and garnish with fresh basil leaves. Serve immediately.

# hearty

a collection of meat & poultry salads

# waldorf chicken salad

**serves 4**

**ingredients**
500 g/1 lb 2 oz red apples, diced
3 tbsp fresh lemon juice
150 ml/5 fl oz mayonnaise
1 head celery
4 shallots, sliced
1 garlic clove, crushed
90 g/3 oz walnuts, chopped
500 g/1 lb 2 oz lean cooked chicken,
    cubed
1 cos lettuce
pepper
chopped walnuts, to garnish

Place the apples in a bowl with the lemon juice and 1 tablespoon of mayonnaise. Leave for 40 minutes or until required.

Slice the celery very thinly. Add the celery with the shallots, garlic and walnuts to the apple, mix and then add the remaining mayonnaise and blend thoroughly.

Add the chicken and mix with the other ingredients.

Line a serving dish with the lettuce. Pile the chicken salad into a serving bowl, sprinkle with pepper and garnish with the chopped walnuts.

# chef's salad

**ingredients**

1 iceberg lettuce, shredded

175 g/6 oz cooked lean ham,
   cut into thin strips

175 g/6 oz cooked tongue,
   cut into thin strips

350 g/12 oz cooked chicken,
   cut into thin strips

175 g/6 oz Gruyère cheese

4 tomatoes, quartered

3 hard-boiled eggs, shelled and quartered

400 ml/14 fl oz Thousand Island dressing

sliced French bread, to serve

Arrange the lettuce on a large serving platter. Arrange the cold meats decoratively on top.

Cut the Gruyère cheese into cubes.

Arrange the cheese cubes over the salad, and the tomato and egg quarters around the edge of the platter. Serve the salad immediately with the Thousand Island dressing and sliced French bread.

# parma ham with melon & asparagus

**ingredients**

225 g/8 oz asparagus spears

1 small or ½ medium-sized Galia or
    cantaloupe melon

55 g/2 oz Parma ham, thinly sliced

150 g/5½ oz bag mixed salad leaves,
    such as herb salad with rocket

85 g/3 oz fresh raspberries

1 tbsp freshly shaved Parmesan cheese

**for the dressing**

1 tbsp balsamic vinegar

2 tbsp raspberry vinegar

2 tbsp orange juice

Trim the asparagus, cutting in half if very long. Cook in lightly salted, boiling water over a medium heat for 5 minutes, or until tender. Drain and plunge into cold water then drain again and reserve.

Cut the melon in half and scoop out the seeds. Cut into small wedges and cut away the rind. Separate the Parma ham slices, cut in half and wrap around the melon wedges.

Arrange the salad leaves on a large serving platter and place the melon wedges on top together with the asparagus spears.

Scatter over the raspberries and Parmesan shavings. Place the vinegars and juice in a screw-top jar and shake until blended. Pour over the salad and serve.

# warm beef niçoise

serves 4

ingredients

4 fillet steaks, about 115 g/4 oz each,
    fat discarded
2 tbsp red wine vinegar
2 tbsp orange juice
2 tsp ready-made English mustard
2 eggs
175 g/6 oz new potatoes
115 g/4 oz green beans, trimmed
175 g/6 oz mixed salad leaves, such as
    baby spinach, rocket and mizuna
1 yellow pepper, peeled, skinned and
    cut into strips
175 g/6 oz cherry tomatoes, halved
black olives, stoned, to garnish (optional)
2 tsp extra-virgin olive oil
pepper

Place the steaks in a shallow dish. Blend the vinegar with
1 tablespoon of orange juice and 1 teaspoon of mustard. Pour
over the steaks, cover and leave in the refrigerator for at least
30 minutes. Turn over halfway through the marinating time.

Place the eggs in a pan and cover with cold water. Bring to the
boil, then reduce the heat to a simmer and cook for 10 minutes.
Remove and plunge the eggs into cold water. Once cold, shell
and reserve.

Meanwhile, place the potatoes in a saucepan and cover with
cold water. Bring to the boil, cover and simmer for 15 minutes,
or until tender when pierced with a fork. Drain and reserve.

Bring a saucepan of water to the boil, add the beans and cook for
5 minutes, or until just tender. Drain, plunge into cold water and
drain again. Arrange the potatoes and beans on top of the salad
leaves together with the yellow pepper, cherry tomatoes and
olives, if using. Blend the remaining orange juice and mustard
with the olive oil and reserve.

Heat a griddle pan until smoking. Drain the steaks and cook for
3–5 minutes on each side or according to personal preference.
Slice the steaks and arrange on top of the salad, then pour over
the dressing and serve.

# cajun chicken salad

**serves 4**

**ingredients**

4 skinless, boneless chicken breasts, about
　　140 g/5 oz each

4 tsp Cajun seasoning

2 tsp sunflower oil (optional)

1 ripe mango, peeled, stoned and
　　cut into thick slices

200 g/7 oz mixed salad leaves

1 red onion, thinly sliced and cut in half

175 g/6 oz cooked beetroot, diced

85 g/3 oz radishes, sliced

55 g/2 oz walnut halves

2 tbsp sesame seeds, to garnish

**for the dressing**

4 tbsp walnut oil

1–2 tsp Dijon mustard

1 tbsp lemon juice

salt and pepper

Make 3 diagonal slashes across each chicken breast. Put the chicken into a shallow dish and sprinkle all over with the Cajun seasoning. Cover and refrigerate for at least 30 minutes.

When ready to cook, brush a griddle pan with the sunflower oil, if using. Heat over a high heat until very hot and a few drops of water sprinkled into the pan sizzle immediately. Add the chicken and cook for 7–8 minutes on each side, or until thoroughly cooked. If still slightly pink in the centre, cook a little longer. Remove the chicken and reserve.

Add the mango slices to the pan and cook for 2 minutes on each side. Remove and reserve.

Meanwhile, arrange the salad leaves in a salad bowl and scatter over the onion, beetroot, radishes and walnut halves.

Put the walnut oil, mustard, lemon juice and salt and pepper to taste in a screw-top jar and shake until well blended. Pour over the salad.

Arrange the mango and the salad on the serving plate, top with the chicken breast and sprinkle with sesame seeds.

# roast beef salad

**serves 4**

**ingredients**

750 g/1 lb 10 oz beef fillet, trimmed
   of any visible fat

pepper, to taste

2 tsp Worcestershire sauce

3 tbsp olive oil

400 g/14 oz green beans

100 g/3½ oz small pasta,
   such as orecchiette

2 red onions, finely sliced

1 large head radicchio

50 g/1¾ oz green olives, stoned

50 g/1¾ oz shelled hazelnuts, whole

**for the dressing**

1 tsp Dijon mustard

2 tbsp white wine vinegar

5 tbsp olive oil

Preheat the oven to 220°C/425°F/Gas Mark 7. Rub the beef with pepper to taste and Worcestershire sauce. Heat 2 tablespoons of the oil in a small roasting tin over a high heat, add the beef and sear on all sides. Transfer the dish to the preheated oven and roast for 30 minutes. Remove and leave to cool.

Bring a large saucepan of water to the boil, add the beans and cook for 5 minutes, or until just tender. Remove with a slotted spoon and refresh the beans under cold running water. Drain and put into a large bowl.

Return the bean cooking water to the boil, add the pasta and cook for 11 minutes, or until tender. Drain, return to the saucepan and toss with the remaining oil.

Add the pasta to the beans with the onions, radicchio leaves, olives and hazelnuts, mix gently and transfer to a serving bowl or dish.  Arrange some thinly sliced beef on top.

Whisk the dressing ingredients together in a separate bowl, then pour over the salad and serve immediately with extra sliced beef.

# walnut, pear & crispy bacon salad

**serves 4**

**ingredients**

4 lean bacon rashers

75 g/2¾ oz walnut halves

2 Red William pears, cored and
   sliced lengthways

1 tbsp lemon juice

175 g/6 oz watercress,
   tough stalks removed

**for the dressing**

3 tbsp extra virgin olive oil

2 tbsp lemon juice

½ tsp clear honey

salt and pepper

Preheat the grill to high. Arrange the bacon on a foil-lined grill pan and cook under the preheated grill until well browned and crisp. Set aside to cool, then cut into 1-cm/½-inch pieces.

Meanwhile, heat a dry frying pan over a medium heat and lightly toast the walnuts, shaking the pan frequently, for 3 minutes, or until lightly browned. Set aside to cool.

Toss the pears in the lemon juice to prevent discoloration. Put the watercress, walnuts, pears and bacon into a salad bowl.

To make the dressing, whisk the oil, lemon juice and honey together in a small bowl or jug. Season to taste with salt and pepper, then pour over the salad. Toss well to combine and serve.

# warm chicken liver salad

**serves 4**

**ingredients**

salad leaves

1 tbsp olive oil

1 small onion, chopped finely

450 g/1 lb frozen chicken livers, thawed

1 tsp chopped fresh tarragon

1 tsp wholegrain mustard

2 tbsp balsamic vinegar

salt and pepper

Arrange the salad leaves on serving plates.

Heat the oil in a non-stick frying pan, add the onion and cook for 5 minutes, or until softened. Add the chicken livers, tarragon and mustard and cook for 3–5 minutes, stirring, until tender. Put on top of the salad leaves.

Add the vinegar, salt and pepper to the pan and heat, stirring all the time, until all the sediment has been lifted from the pan. Pour over the chicken livers and serve warm.

# artichoke & parma ham salad

**serves 4**

**ingredients**

275 g/9¾ oz canned artichoke
    hearts in oil, drained

4 small tomatoes

25 g/1 oz sun-dried tomatoes in oil,
    drained

40 g/1½ oz Parma ham

25 g/1 oz stoned black olives, halved

handful of fresh basil sprigs

crusty bread, to serve

**for the dressing**

3 tbsp olive oil

1 tbsp white wine vinegar

1 garlic clove, crushed

½ tsp mild mustard

1 tsp clear honey

salt and pepper, to taste

Make sure the artichoke hearts are thoroughly drained, then cut them into quarters and put into a serving bowl. Cut each fresh tomato into wedges. Slice the sun-dried tomatoes into thin strips. Cut the Parma ham into thin strips and add to the bowl with the tomatoes and olive halves.

Keeping a few basil sprigs whole for garnishing, tear the remainder of the leaves into small pieces and add to the bowl containing the other salad ingredients.

To make the dressing, put all the ingredients into a screw-top jar and shake vigorously until they are well blended.

Pour the dressing over the salad and toss together. Garnish the salad with a few basil sprigs and serve with crusty bread.

# butter bean, onion & herb salad with spicy sausage

**serves 2**

**ingredients**

1 tbsp sunflower oil

1 small onion, finely sliced

250 g/9 oz canned butter beans,
  drained and rinsed

1 tsp balsamic vinegar

2 chorizo sausages, sliced diagonally

1 small tomato, diced

2 tbsp harissa paste

85 g/3 oz mixed herb salad

Heat the oil in a non-stick frying pan over a medium heat, add the onion and cook, stirring frequently, until softened but not browned. Add the beans and cook for a further 1 minute, then add the vinegar, stirring well. Keep warm.

Meanwhile, heat a separate dry frying pan over a medium heat, add the chorizo slices and cook, turning occasionally, until lightly browned. Remove with a slotted spoon and drain on kitchen paper.

Mix the tomato and harissa paste together in a small bowl. Divide the herb salad between 2 plates, spoon over the bean mixture and scatter over the warm chorizo slices. Top with a spoonful of the tomato and harissa mixture and serve immediately.

# turkey & rice salad

serves 4

**ingredients**

1 litre/1¾ pints chicken stock
175 g/6 oz mixed long-grain and wild rice
2 tbsp sunflower or corn oil
225 g/8 oz skinless, boneless turkey
    breast, trimmed of all visible fat and
    cut into thin strips
225 g/8 oz mangetout
115 g/4 oz oyster mushrooms,
    torn into pieces
55 g/2 oz shelled pistachio nuts,
    finely chopped
2 tbsp chopped fresh coriander
1 tbsp snipped fresh garlic chives
salt and pepper
1 tbsp balsamic vinegar
fresh garlic chives, to garnish

Reserve 3 tablespoons of the chicken stock and bring the remainder to the boil in a large saucepan. Add the rice and cook for 30 minutes, or until tender. Drain and leave to cool slightly.

Meanwhile, heat 1 tablespoon of the oil in a preheated wok or frying pan. Stir-fry the turkey over a medium heat for 3–4 minutes, or until cooked through. Using a slotted spoon, transfer the turkey to a dish. Add the mangetout and mushrooms to the wok and stir-fry for 1 minute. Add the reserved stock, bring to the boil, then reduce the heat, cover and simmer for 3–4 minutes. Transfer the vegetables to the dish and leave to cool slightly.

Thoroughly mix the rice, turkey, mangetout, mushrooms, nuts, coriander and garlic chives together, then season to taste with salt and pepper. Drizzle with the remaining sunflower oil and the vinegar and garnish with fresh garlic chives. Serve warm.

# smoked chicken & cranberry salad

serves 4

**ingredients**

1 smoked chicken, weighing 1.3 kg/3 lb

115 g/4 oz dried cranberries

2 tbsp apple juice or water

200 g/7 oz sugar snap peas

2 ripe avocados

juice of ½ lemon

4 lettuce hearts

1 bunch watercress, trimmed

55 g/2 oz rocket

**for the dressing**

2 tbsp olive oil

1 tbsp walnut oil

2 tbsp lemon juice

1 tbsp chopped fresh mixed herbs,
    such as parsley and lemon thyme

salt and pepper

Carve the chicken carefully, slicing the white meat. Divide the legs into thighs and drumsticks and trim the wings. Cover with clingfilm and refrigerate.

Put the cranberries in a bowl. Stir in the apple juice, cover with clingfilm and leave to soak for 30 minutes.

Meanwhile, blanch the sugar snap peas, refresh under cold running water and drain.

Peel, stone and slice the avocados, then toss in the lemon juice to prevent discoloration.

Separate the lettuce hearts and arrange on a large serving platter with the avocados, sugar snap peas, watercress, rocket and the chicken.

Put all the dressing ingredients, with salt and pepper to taste, in a screw-top jar, screw on the lid and shake until well blended.

Drain the cranberries and mix them with the dressing, then pour over the salad. Serve immediately.

# melon, chorizo & artichoke salad

**serves 8**

**ingredients**

12 small globe artichokes

juice of ½ lemon

2 tbsp Spanish olive oil

1 small orange-fleshed melon,
    such as cantaloupe

200 g/7 oz chorizo sausage,
    outer casing removed

fresh tarragon or flat-leaf parsley sprigs,
    to garnish

**for the dressing**

3 tbsp Spanish extra-virgin olive oil

1 tbsp red wine vinegar

1 tsp prepared mustard

1 tbsp chopped fresh tarragon

salt and pepper

Cut the artichokes into quarters and brush with lemon juice to prevent discoloration.

Heat the olive oil in a large, heavy-based frying pan. Add the prepared artichokes and fry, stirring frequently, for 5 minutes, or until the artichoke leaves are golden brown. Remove from the frying pan, transfer to a large serving bowl and leave to cool.

To prepare the melon, cut in half and scoop out the seeds with a spoon. Cut the flesh into bite-sized cubes. Add to the cooled artichokes. Cut the chorizo into bite-sized chunks and add to the melon and artichokes.

To make the dressing, place all the ingredients in a small bowl and whisk together. Just before serving, pour the dressing over the prepared salad ingredients and toss together. Serve the salad garnished with tarragon or parsley sprigs.

# layered chicken salad

serves 4

ingredients
750 g/1 lb 10 oz new potatoes, scrubbed
1 red pepper, halved and deseeded
1 green pepper, halved and deseeded
2 small courgettes, sliced
1 small onion, thinly sliced
3 tomatoes, sliced
350 g/12 oz cooked chicken, sliced
snipped fresh chives, to garnish

for the dressing
150 ml/5 fl oz natural yogurt
3 tbsp mayonnaise
1 tbsp snipped fresh chives
salt and pepper

Put the potatoes into a large saucepan, add just enough cold water to cover and bring to the boil. Lower the heat, cover and simmer for 15–20 minutes until tender. Meanwhile, place the pepper halves, skin side up, under a preheated hot grill and grill until the skins blacken and begin to char.

Remove the peppers with tongs, place in a bowl and cover with clingfilm. Set aside until cool enough to handle, then peel off the skins and slice the flesh.

Bring a small pan of lightly salted water to the boil. Add the courgettes, bring back to the boil and simmer for 3 minutes. Drain, rinse under cold running water to prevent any further cooking and drain again. Set aside.

To make the dressing, whisk the yogurt, mayonnaise and snipped chives together in a small bowl until well blended. Season to taste with salt and pepper.

When the potatoes are tender, drain, cool and slice them. Add them to the dressing and mix gently to coat evenly. Spoon the potatoes on to 4 serving plates, dividing them equally.

Top each plate with one quarter of the pepper slices and courgettes. Layer one quarter of the onion and tomato slices, then the sliced chicken, on top of each serving. Garnish with snipped fresh chives and serve immediately.

# rare roast beef pasta salad

**ingredients**

450 g/1 lb rump or sirloin steak
　in a single piece
salt and pepper
450 g/1 lb dried fusilli
4 tbsp olive oil
2 tbsp lime juice
2 tbsp Thai fish sauce
2 tsp clear honey
4 spring onions, sliced
1 cucumber, peeled and cut into
　2.5 cm/1 inch chunks
3 tomatoes, cut into wedges
1 tbsp finely chopped fresh mint

Season the steak with salt and pepper. Grill or pan-fry it for 4 minutes on each side. Allow to rest for 5 minutes, then slice thinly across the grain.

Meanwhile, bring a large saucepan of lightly salted water to the boil. Add the pasta, bring back to the boil and cook for 8–10 minutes or until tender, but still firm to the bite. Drain the fusilli, refresh in cold water and drain again thoroughly. Toss the fusilli in the olive oil and set aside until required.

Combine the lime juice, fish sauce and honey in a small saucepan and cook over a medium heat for 2 minutes.

Add the spring onions, cucumber, tomatoes and mint to the pan, then add the steak and mix well. Season to taste with salt.

Transfer the fusilli to a large, warm serving dish and top with the steak and salad mixture. Serve just warm or allow to cool completely.

# roast duck salad

serves 4

**ingredients**

2 duck breasts

2 Little Gem lettuces, shredded

115 g/4 oz beansprouts

1 yellow pepper, deseeded and
    cut into thin strips

½ cucumber, deseeded and
    cut into matchsticks

2 tsp shredded lime zest

2 tbsp shredded coconut, toasted

**for the dressing**

juice of 2 limes

3 tbsp fish sauce

1 tbsp soft brown sugar

2 tsp sweet chilli sauce

2.5 cm/1 inch fresh root ginger,
    grated finely

3 tbsp chopped fresh mint

3 tbsp chopped fresh basil

Preheat the oven to 200°C/400°F/ Gas Mark 6. Place the duck breasts on a rack set over a roasting tin and roast in the oven for 20–30 minutes, or until cooked as desired and the skin is crisp. Remove from the oven and set aside to cool.

In a large bowl, combine the lettuce, beansprouts, pepper and cucumber. Cut the cooled duck into slices and add to the salad. Mix well.

In a bowl, whisk together the lime juice, fish sauce, sugar, chilli sauce, ginger, mint and basil. Add the dressing to the salad and toss well.

Turn the salad out onto a serving platter and garnish with the lime zest and shredded coconut before serving.

# warm mushroom, spinach & pancetta salad

**ingredients**

275 g/9¾ oz fresh baby spinach leaves

2 tbsp olive oil

150 g/5½ oz pancetta

280 g/10 oz mixed wild mushrooms, sliced

**for the dressing**

5 tbsp olive oil

1 tbsp balsamic vinegar

1 tsp Dijon mustard

pinch of sugar

salt and pepper

To make the dressing, place the olive oil, vinegar, mustard, sugar, salt and pepper in a small bowl and whisk together. Rinse the baby spinach under cold running water, then drain and place in a large salad bowl.

Heat the oil in a large frying pan. Add the pancetta and fry for 3 minutes. Add the mushrooms and cook for 3–4 minutes, or until tender.

Pour the dressing into the frying pan and immediately turn the fried mixture and dressing into the bowl with the spinach. Toss until coated with the dressing and serve immediately.

# crispy spinach & bacon

**serves 4**

**ingredients**

4 tbsp olive oil

4 rashers of streaky bacon, diced

1 thick slice of white bread,
   crusts removed, cut into cubes

450 g/1 lb fresh spinach, torn or shredded

Heat 2 tablespoons of the olive oil over a high heat in a large frying pan. Add the diced bacon to the pan and cook for 3–4 minutes, or until crisp. Remove with a slotted spoon, draining carefully, and set aside.

Toss the cubes of bread in the fat remaining in the pan over a high heat for about 4 minutes, or until crisp and golden. Remove the croûtons with a slotted spoon, draining carefully, and set them aside.

Add the remaining oil to the frying pan and heat. Toss the spinach in the oil over a high heat for about 3 minutes, or until it has just wilted. Turn into a serving bowl and sprinkle with the bacon and croûtons. Serve immediately.

# thai-style chicken salad

**serves 4**

**ingredients**

400 g/14 oz small new potatoes,
  scrubbed and halved lengthways
200 g/7 oz baby corn cobs
150 g/5½ oz beansprouts
3 spring onions, trimmed and sliced
4 cooked, skinless chicken breasts, sliced
1 tbsp chopped lemon grass
2 tbsp chopped fresh coriander
salt and pepper
wedges of lime, to garnish
fresh coriander leaves, to garnish

**for the dressing**

6 tbsp chilli oil or sesame oil
2 tbsp lime juice
1 tbsp light soy sauce
1 tbsp chopped fresh coriander
1 small, red chilli, deseeded and
  finely sliced

Bring two saucepans of water to the boil. Put the potatoes into one saucepan and cook for 15 minutes until tender. Put the corn cobs into the other saucepan and cook for 5 minutes until tender. Drain the potatoes and corn cobs well and leave to cool.

When the vegetables are cool, transfer them into a large serving dish. Add the beansprouts, spring onions, chicken, lemon grass and coriander and season with salt and pepper.

To make the dressing, put all the ingredients into a screw-top jar and shake well. Alternatively, put them into a bowl and mix together well. Drizzle the dressing over the salad and garnish with lime wedges and coriander leaves. Serve at once.

# duckling & radish salad

**ingredients**

350 g/12 oz boneless duckling breasts

2 tbsp plain flour

salt and pepper

1 egg

2 tbsp water

2 tbsp sesame seeds

3 tbsp sesame oil

1/2 head Chinese leaves, shredded

3 celery sticks, sliced finely

8 radishes, trimmed and halved

fresh basil leaves, to garnish

**for the dressing**

finely grated rind of 1 lime

2 tbsp lime juice

2 tbsp olive oil

1 tbsp light soy sauce

1 tbsp chopped fresh basil

salt and pepper

Put each duckling breast between sheets of greaseproof paper or clingfilm. Use a meat mallet or rolling pin to beat them out and flatten them slightly.

Sprinkle the flour onto a large plate and season with salt and pepper. Beat the egg and water together in a shallow bowl, then sprinkle the sesame seeds on to a separate plate.

Dip the duckling breasts first into the seasoned flour, then into the egg mixture and finally into the sesame seeds, to coat the duckling evenly. Heat the sesame oil in a preheated wok or large frying pan.

Fry the duckling breasts over a medium heat for about 8 minutes, turning once. To test whether they are cooked, insert a sharp knife into the thickest part – the juices should run clear. Lift them out and drain on kitchen paper.

To make the dressing for the salad, whisk together the lime rind and juice, olive oil, soy sauce and chopped basil. Season with a little salt and pepper.

Arrange the Chinese leaves, celery and radish on a serving plate. Slice the duckling breasts thinly and place on top of the salad. Drizzle with the dressing and garnish with fresh basil leaves. Serve at once.

# chicken, cheese & rocket salad

serves 4

**ingredients**

150 g/5½ oz rocket leaves

2 celery sticks, trimmed and sliced

½ cucumber, sliced

2 spring onions, trimmed and sliced

2 tbsp chopped fresh parsley

25 g/1 oz walnut pieces

350 g/12 oz boneless roast chicken, sliced

125 g/4½ oz Stilton cheese, cubed

handful of seedless red grapes,
    halved (optional)

salt and pepper

**for the dressing**

2 tbsp olive oil

1 tbsp sherry vinegar

1 tsp Dijon mustard

1 tbsp chopped mixed herbs

Wash the rocket leaves, pat dry with kitchen paper and put them into a large salad bowl. Add the celery, cucumber, spring onions, parsley and walnuts and mix together well. Transfer onto a large serving platter. Arrange the chicken slices over the salad, then scatter over the cheese. Add the red grapes, if using. Season well with salt and pepper.

To make the dressing, put all the ingredients into a screw-top jar and shake well. Alternatively, put them into a bowl and mix together well. Drizzle the dressing over the salad and serve.

# grilled lamb with
# yogurt & herb dressing

**serves 4**

**ingredients**

2 tbsp sunflower oil, plus extra
    for grilling the lamb
1 tbsp tomato pureé
½ tbsp ground cumin
1 tsp lemon juice
1 garlic clove, crushed
pinch of cayenne pepper
salt and pepper
500 g/1 lb 2 oz lamb neck fillets,
    trimmed with excess fat removed
toasted sesame seeds and chopped
    fresh parsley, to garnish

**for the dressing**

2 tbsp fresh lemon juice
1 tsp clear honey
75 g/3 oz Greek yogurt
2 tbsp finely shredded fresh mint
2 tbsp chopped fresh parsley
1 tbsp finely snipped fresh chives
salt and pepper

Mix the 2 tablespoons oil, tomato pureé, cumin, lemon juice, garlic, cayenne and salt and pepper to taste together in a non-metallic bowl. Add the lamb fillets and rub all over with the marinade. Cover the bowl and marinate in the fridge for at least 2 hours, but ideally overnight.

Meanwhile, to make the dressing, whisk the lemon juice and honey together until the honey dissolves. Whisk in the yogurt until well blended. Stir in the herbs and add salt and pepper to taste. Cover and chill until required.

Remove the lamb from the fridge 15 minutes before you are ready to cook. Heat the grill to its highest setting and lightly brush the grill rack with oil. Grill the lamb fillet, turning it once, for 10 minutes for medium and 12 minutes for well done. Leave the lamb to cool completely, then cover and chill until required.

Thinly slice the lamb fillets, then divide between 4 plates. Adjust the seasoning in the dressing, if necessary, then spoon over the lamb slices. Sprinkle with toasted sesame seeds and parsley and serve.

# smoked chicken salad with avocado & tarragon dressing

serves 4 – 6

**ingredients**

2 large, juicy beef tomatoes, sliced

600 g/1 lb 5 oz smoked chicken, skinned
    and cut into slices

250 g/9 oz fresh watercress, any thick
    stems or yellow leaves removed,
    then rinsed and patted dry

75 g/3 oz fresh beansprouts, soaked for
    20 minutes in cold water, then drained
    well and patted dry

leaves from several sprigs fresh flat-leaf
    parsley or coriander

**for the dressing**

1 ripe, soft avocado

2 tbsp lemon juice

1 tbsp tarragon vinegar

75 g/3 oz Greek yogurt

1 small garlic clove, crushed

1 tbsp chopped fresh tarragon leaves

salt and pepper

To make the dressing, put the avocado, lemon juice and vinegar in a blender or food processor and blend until smooth, scraping down the side with a rubber spatula. Add the yogurt, garlic and tarragon leaves and process again. Season with salt and pepper to taste, then transfer to a bowl. Cover closely with clingfilm and chill for 2 hours.

To assemble the salad, divide the tomato slices between 4–6 individual plates. Toss the smoked chicken, watercress, beansprouts and parsley or coriander leaves together. Divide the salad ingredients between the plates.

Adjust the seasoning in the dressing, if necessary. Spoon the dressing over each salad and serve.

# roast pork & pumpkin salad

**serves 4 – 6**

**ingredients**

1 small pumpkin, about 1.6 kg/3½ lb,
  cut in half and seeded

2 red onions, cut into wedges

olive oil

100 g/3½ oz green beans, topped and
  tailed and cut in half

600 g/1 lb 5 oz roast pork, any skin or rind
  removed and cut into bite-sized chunks

large handful of fresh rocket leaves

100 g/3½ oz feta cheese, drained and
  crumbled

2 tbsp toasted pine kernels

2 tbsp chopped fresh parsley

salt and pepper

**for the vinaigrette**

6 tbsp extra-virgin olive oil

3 tbsp balsamic vinegar

½ tsp sugar

½ tsp Dijon, prepared English or
  wholegrain mustard

salt and pepper

Preheat the oven to 200°C/400°F/Gas Mark 6. Cut the pumpkin in half, scoop out the seeds and fibres and cut the flesh into wedges about 4 cm/1½ inches wide. Very lightly rub the pumpkin and onion wedges with the olive oil, place in a roasting pan and roast for 25–30 minutes until the pumpkin and onions are tender but holding their shape.

Meanwhile, bring a small pan of salted water to the boil. Add the green beans and blanch for 5 minutes, or until tender. Drain well and cool under cold running water to stop the cooking. Drain well and pat dry.

Remove the pumpkin and onion wedges from the oven as soon as they are tender-crisp and leave to cool completely. When the pumpkin is cool, peel and cut into bite-sized pieces.

To make the vinaigrette, put the oil, vinegar, sugar, mustard and salt and pepper to taste into a screw-top jar and shake until blended.

To assemble the salad, put the pumpkins, onions, beans, pork, rocket, feta, pine kernels and parsley in a large bowl and gently toss together – be careful not to break up the pumpkin. Shake the dressing again, pour over the salad and gently toss. Divide between individual bowls and serve.

# roast chicken with pesto cream salad

**serves 4 – 6**

**ingredients**

600 g/1 lb 5 oz cooked boneless chicken,
   any skin removed and cut into
   bite-sized pieces

3 celery sticks, chopped

2 large skinned red peppers from a jar,
   well drained and sliced

salt and pepper

iceberg lettuce leaves, to serve

**for the pesto cream**

150 ml/5 fl oz crème fraîche or soured
   cream

about 4 tbsp bottled pesto sauce

To make the pesto cream, put the crème fraîche into a large bowl, then beat in 4 tablespoons pesto sauce. Taste and add more pesto if you want a stronger flavour.

Add the chicken, celery and red peppers to the bowl and gently toss together. Add salt and pepper to taste and toss again. Cover and chill until required.

Remove the salad from the fridge 10 minutes before serving to return to room temperature. Give the salad ingredients a good stir, then divide between individual plates lined with lettuce leaves.

# sparkling
a collection of fish and seafood salads

# salad niçoise

serves 4

**ingredients**

2 tuna steaks, about 2 cm/¾ inch thick

olive oil

salt and pepper

250 g/9 oz green beans, topped and tailed

125 ml/4 fl oz vinaigrette or garlic
    vinaigrette dressing

2 hearts of lettuce, leaves separated

3 large hard-boiled eggs, quartered

2 juicy vine-ripened tomatoes,
    cut into wedges

50 g/1¾ oz anchovy fillets in oil, drained

55 g/2 oz Niçoise olives, stoned

Heat a ridged cast-iron griddle pan over a high heat until you can feel the heat rising from the surface. Brush the tuna steaks with oil, place oiled side down on the hot pan, and chargrill for 2 minutes. Lightly brush the top side of the tuna steaks with more oil. Use a pair of tongs to turn the tuna steaks over, then season to taste with salt and pepper. Continue chargrilling for a further 2 minutes for rare or up to 4 minutes for well done. Leave to cool.

Meanwhile, bring a saucepan of salted water to the boil. Add the beans to the pan and return to the boil, then boil for 3 minutes, or until tender-crisp. Drain the beans and immediately transfer them to a large bowl. Pour over the vinaigrette and stir together, then leave the beans to cool in the dressing.

To serve, line a platter with lettuce leaves. Lift the beans out of the bowl, leaving the excess dressing behind, and pile them in the centre of the platter. Break the tuna into large pieces and arrange it over the beans. Arrange the hard-boiled eggs and tomatoes around the side. Place the anchovy fillets over the salad, then scatter with the olives. Drizzle the remaining dressing in the bowl over everything and serve.

# lentil & tuna salad

**serves 4**

**ingredients**
2 ripe tomatoes
1 small red onion
400 g/14 oz can lentils, drained
185 g/6½ oz can tuna, drained
2 tbsp chopped fresh coriander
pepper

**for the dressing**
3 tbsp virgin olive oil
1 tbsp lemon juice
1 tsp wholegrain mustard
1 garlic clove, crushed
½ tsp ground cumin
½ tsp ground coriander

Using a sharp knife, deseed the tomatoes and then chop them into fine dice. Finely chop the red onion.

To make the dressing, whisk together the virgin olive oil, lemon juice, mustard, garlic, cumin and ground coriander in a small bowl until thoroughly combined. Set aside until required.

Mix together the chopped onion, diced tomatoes and drained lentils in a large bowl.

Flake the tuna with a fork and stir it into the onion, tomato and lentil mixture. Stir in the chopped fresh coriander and mix well.

Pour the dressing over the lentil and tuna salad and season with pepper to taste. Serve immediately.

# tuna & two-bean salad

**ingredients**

200 g/7 oz green beans

400 g/14 oz canned small white beans,
    such as cannellini, rinsed and drained

4 spring onions, finely chopped

2 fresh tuna steaks, about 225 g/8 oz each
    and 2 cm/¾ inch thick

olive oil, for brushing

salt and pepper

250 g/9 oz cherry tomatoes, halved

lettuce leaves

fresh mint and parsley sprigs, to garnish

**for the dressing**

handful of fresh mint leaves, shredded

handful of fresh parsley leaves, chopped

1 garlic clove, crushed

4 tbsp extra-virgin olive oil

1 tbsp red wine vinegar

salt and pepper

First, make the dressing. Put the mint leaves, parsley leaves, garlic, olive oil and vinegar into a screw-top jar, add salt and pepper to taste and shake until blended. Pour into a large bowl and set aside.

Bring a saucepan of lightly salted water to the boil. Add the green beans and cook for 3 minutes. Add the white beans and cook for a further 4 minutes until the green beans are tender-crisp and the white beans are heated through. Drain well and add to the bowl with the dressing and spring onions. Toss together.

To cook the tuna, heat a ridged griddle pan over a high heat. Lightly brush the tuna steaks with oil, then season to taste with salt and pepper. Cook the steaks for 2 minutes, then turn over and cook on the other side for a further 2 minutes for rare or up to 4 minutes for well done.

Remove the tuna from the griddle pan and leave to rest for 2 minutes, or alternatively leave until completely cool. When ready to serve, add the tomatoes to the bean mixture and toss lightly. Line a serving platter with lettuce leaves and pile on the bean salad. Place the tuna over the top. Serve warm or at room temperature, garnished with the herbs.

122     sparkling – a collection of fish & seafood salads

# tuna & fresh vegetable salad

**serves 4**

**ingredients**

12 cherry tomatoes, halved

225 g/8 oz whole green beans,
    cut into 2.5 cm/1 inch pieces

225 g/8 oz courgettes, sliced thinly

225 g/8 oz button mushrooms, sliced thinly

salad leaves

350 g/12 oz canned tuna in brine,
    drained and flaked

fresh parsley, to garnish

**for the dressing**

4 tbsp mayonnaise

4 tbsp natural yogurt

2 tbsp white wine vinegar

salt and pepper

To make the dressing, put the mayonnaise, yogurt, vinegar, salt and pepper in a screw-topped jar and shake together until the ingredients are well blended.

Put the tomatoes, beans, courgettes and mushrooms in a bowl. Pour over the dressing and leave to marinate for about 1 hour.

Arrange the salad leaves on a serving dish. Add the vegetables and then the tuna and garnish with parsley.

# prawn & mango salad

**serves 4**

**ingredients**

2 mangoes

225 g/8 oz peeled, cooked prawns

salad leaves, to serve

4 whole cooked prawns, to garnish

**for the dressing**

juice from the mangoes

6 tbsp natural yogurt

2 tbsp mayonnaise

1 tbsp lemon juice

salt and pepper

Cutting close to the stone, cut a large slice from one side of each mango, then cut another slice from the opposite side. Without breaking the skin, cut the flesh in the segments into squares, then push the skin inside out to expose the cubes and cut away from the skin. Use a sharp knife to peel the remaining centre section and cut the flesh away from the stone into cubes. Reserve any juice in a bowl and put the mango flesh in a separate bowl.

Add the prawns to the mango flesh. To the juice, add the yogurt, mayonnaise, lemon juice, salt and pepper and blend together.

Arrange the salad leaves on a serving dish and add the mango flesh and prawns. Pour over the dressing and serve garnished with the whole prawns.

# salmon & avocado salad

serves 4

ingredients

450 g/1 lb new potatoes

4 salmon steaks, about 115 g/4 oz each

1 avocado

juice of ½ lemon

55 g/2 oz baby spinach leaves

125 g/4½ oz mixed small salad leaves,
    including watercress

12 cherry tomatoes, halved

55 g/2 oz chopped walnuts

for the dressing

3 tbsp unsweetened clear apple juice

1 tsp balsamic vinegar

freshly ground black pepper

Cut the new potatoes into bite-sized pieces, put into a saucepan and cover with cold water. Bring to the boil, then reduce the heat, cover and simmer for 10–15 minutes, or until just tender. Drain and keep warm.

Meanwhile, preheat the grill to medium. Cook the salmon steaks under the preheated grill for 10–15 minutes, depending on the thickness of the steaks, turning halfway through cooking. Remove from the grill and keep warm.

While the potatoes and salmon are cooking, cut the avocado in half, remove and discard the stone and peel the flesh. Cut the avocado flesh into slices and coat in the lemon juice to prevent it from discolouring.

Toss the spinach leaves and mixed salad leaves together in a large serving bowl until combined, then divide between 4 serving plates. Arrange 6 cherry tomato halves on each plate of salad.

Remove and discard the skin and any bones from the salmon. Flake the salmon and divide between the plates along with the potatoes. Sprinkle the walnuts over the salads.

To make the dressing, mix the apple juice and vinegar together in a small bowl or jug and season well with pepper. Drizzle over the salads and serve immediately.

# coconut prawns with cucumber salad

**serves 4**

**ingredients**

200 g/7 oz brown basmati rice

½ tsp coriander seeds

2 egg whites, lightly beaten

100 g/3½ oz unsweetened
   desiccated coconut

24 raw tiger prawns, peeled

½ cucumber

4 spring onions, thinly sliced lengthways

1 tsp sesame oil

1 tbsp finely chopped fresh coriander

Bring a large saucepan of water to the boil, add the rice and cook for 25 minutes, or until tender. Drain and keep in a colander covered with a clean tea towel to absorb the steam.

Meanwhile, soak 8 wooden skewers in cold water for 30 minutes, then drain. Crush the coriander seeds in a mortar with a pestle. Heat a non-stick frying pan over a medium heat, add the crushed coriander seeds and cook, turning, until they begin to colour. Tip onto a plate and set aside.

Put the egg whites into a shallow bowl and the coconut into a separate bowl. Roll each prawn first in the egg whites, then in the coconut. Thread onto a skewer. Repeat so that each skewer is threaded with 3 coated prawns.

Preheat the grill to high. Using a potato peeler, peel long strips from the cucumber to create ribbons, put into a colander to drain, then toss with the spring onions and oil in a bowl and set aside.

Cook the prawns under the preheated grill for 3–4 minutes on each side, or until slightly browned.

Meanwhile, mix the rice with the toasted coriander seeds and fresh coriander and divide this and the cucumber salad between bowls. Serve with the hot prawn skewers.

# tuna & avocado salad

**serves 4**

**ingredients**

2 avocados, stoned, peeled and cubed

250 g/9 oz cherry tomatoes, halved

2 red peppers, deseeded and chopped

flat-leaf parsley

2 garlic cloves, crushed

1 fresh red chilli, deseeded and
    finely chopped

juice of $\frac{1}{2}$ lemon

6 tbsp olive oil

pepper

3 tbsp sesame seeds

4 fresh tuna steaks,
    about 150 g/5$\frac{1}{2}$ oz each

8 cooked new potatoes, cubed

rocket leaves and crusty bread, to serve

Toss the avocados, tomatoes, red peppers, parsley, garlic, chilli,
lemon juice and 2 tablespoons of the oil together in a large bowl.
Season to taste with pepper, cover and chill in the refrigerator for
30 minutes.

Lightly crush the sesame seeds in a mortar with a pestle. Tip the
crushed seeds on to a plate and spread out. Press each tuna
steak in turn into the crushed seeds to coat on both sides.

Heat 2 tablespoons of the remaining oil in a frying pan, add
the potatoes and cook, stirring frequently, for 5–8 minutes, or
until crisp and brown. Remove from the pan and drain on
kitchen paper.

Wipe out the pan, add the remaining oil and heat over a high
heat until very hot. Add the tuna steaks and cook for 3–4 minutes
on each side.

To serve, divide the avocado salad between 4 serving plates.
Top each with a tuna steak, scatter over the potatoes and rocket
leaves and serve with crusty bread.

# tomato, salmon & prawn salad

**serves 4**

**ingredients**

115 g/4 oz cherry or baby plum tomatoes

several lettuce leaves

4 ripe tomatoes, roughly chopped

100 g/3½ oz smoked salmon

200 g/7 oz large cooked prawns,
   thawed if frozen

**for the dressing**

1 tbsp Dijon mustard

2 tsp caster sugar

2 tsp red wine vinegar

2 tbsp medium olive oil

few fresh dill sprigs, plus extra to garnish

pepper

Halve most of the cherry tomatoes. Place the lettuce leaves around the edge of a shallow bowl and add all the tomatoes and cherry tomatoes. Using scissors, snip the smoked salmon into strips and scatter over the tomatoes, then add the prawns.

Mix the mustard, sugar, vinegar and oil together in a small bowl, then tear most of the dill sprigs into it. Mix well and pour over the salad. Toss well to coat the salad with the dressing. Snip the remaining dill over the top and season to taste with pepper.

# lobster salad

**ingredients**

2 raw lobster tails

radicchio leaves

fresh dill sprigs, to garnish

**for the mayonnaise**

1 large lemon

1 large egg yolk

½ tsp Dijon mustard

150 ml/5 fl oz olive oil

salt and pepper

1 tbsp chopped fresh dill

To make the lemon-dill mayonnaise, finely grate half the lemon rind and squeeze the juice. Beat the egg yolk in a small bowl, then beat in the mustard and 1 teaspoon of the lemon juice.

Using a balloon whisk or electric mixer, beat the oil into the egg yolk mixture, drop by drop, until a thick mayonnaise forms. Stir in the lemon rind and 1 tablespoon of the remaining lemon juice.

Season the mayonnaise to taste with salt and pepper and add more lemon juice if desired. Stir in the dill, cover and chill in the refrigerator until required.

Bring a large saucepan of lightly salted water to the boil. Add the lobster tails, return to the boil and cook for 6 minutes, or until the flesh is opaque and the shells are red. Drain immediately and set aside to cool.

Remove the lobster flesh from the shells and cut into bite-sized pieces. Arrange the radicchio leaves on individual plates and top with the lobster flesh. Place a spoonful of the lemon-dill mayonnaise on the side. Garnish with dill sprigs and serve.

# russian salad

serves 4

ingredients

115 g/4 oz new potatoes

115 g/4 oz frozen or shelled
   fresh broad beans

115 g/4 oz baby carrots

115 g/4 oz baby sweetcorn

115 g/4 oz baby turnips

115 g/4 oz button mushrooms,
   cut into thin batons

350 g/12 oz cooked peeled prawns,
   deveined

125 ml/4 fl oz mayonnaise

1 tbsp lemon juice

2 tbsp bottled capers, drained and rinsed

salt and pepper

2 tbsp extra-virgin olive oil

2 hard-boiled eggs, shelled and halved

4 canned anchovy fillets, drained
   and halved

paprika, to garnish

Cook the potatoes, broad beans, carrots, sweetcorn and turnips simultaneously. Cook the potatoes in a large saucepan of lightly salted boiling water for 20 minutes. Cook the broad beans in a small saucepan of lightly salted water for 3 minutes, then drain, refresh under cold running water and reserve. Cook the carrots, sweetcorn and turnips in a large saucepan of lightly salted boiling water for 6 minutes.

Mix the mushrooms and prawns together in a bowl. Mix the mayonnaise and lemon juice together in a separate bowl, then fold half the mixture into the prawn mixture. Fold in the capers and season to taste with salt and pepper.

Drain the mixed vegetables, refresh under cold running water and tip into a bowl. When the potatoes are cooked, drain, refresh under cold running water and tip into the bowl. Pop the broad beans out of their skins by pinching them between your finger and thumb and add to the bowl. Add the olive oil and toss to coat. Divide the potatoes and vegetables between serving plates and top with the prawn mixture. Place a hard-boiled egg half in the centre of each and garnish with the halved anchovies. Dust the eggs with paprika and serve with the remaining mayonnaise mixture.

# seafood salad

**serves 4**

**ingredients**

250 g/9 oz live mussels

350 g/12 oz live scallops, shucked
and cleaned

250 g/9 oz prepared squid, cut into rings
and tentacles

1 red onion, halved and finely sliced

chopped parsley, to serve

lemon wedges, to serve

**for the dressing**

4 tbsp extra-virgin olive oil

2 tbsp white wine vinegar

1 tbsp lemon juice

1 garlic clove, finely chopped

1 tbsp chopped fresh flat-leaf parsley

salt and pepper

Clean the mussels by scrubbing or scraping the shells and
pulling out any beards that are attached to them. Discard any
with broken shells or any that refuse to close when tapped. Put
the mussels in a colander and rinse well under cold running
water. Put them in a large saucepan with a little water and cook,
covered, over a high heat, shaking the saucepan occasionally,
for 3–4 minutes, or until the mussels have opened. Discard any
mussels that remain closed. Strain the mussels, reserving the
cooking liquid. Refresh the mussels under cold running water,
drain and set aside.

Return the reserved cooking liquid to the saucepan and bring
to the boil, add the scallops and squid and cook for 3 minutes.
Remove from the heat and drain. Refresh under cold running
water and drain again. Remove the mussels from their shells. Put
them in a bowl with the scallops and squid and leave to cool.
Cover with clingfilm and chill in the refrigerator for 45 minutes.

Divide the seafood between 4 serving plates and top with the
onion. Combine all the dressing ingredients in a small bowl,
then drizzle over the salad. Garnish with chopped parsley and
lemon wedges to serve.

# cantaloupe & crab salad

**serves 4**

**ingredients**

350 g/12 oz fresh crabmeat

5 tbsp mayonnaise

50 ml/2 fl oz natural yogurt

4 tsp extra-virgin olive oil

4 tsp lime juice

1 spring onion, finely chopped

4 tsp finely chopped fresh parsley

pinch of cayenne pepper

1 cantaloupe melon

2 radicchio heads, separated into leaves

fresh parsley sprigs, to garnish

crusty bread, to serve

Place the crabmeat in a large bowl and pick over it very carefully to remove any remaining shell or cartilage, but try not to break the meat up.

Place the mayonnaise, yogurt, olive oil, lime juice, spring onion, chopped fresh parsley and cayenne pepper into a separate bowl and mix until thoroughly blended. Fold in the crabmeat.

Cut the melon in half and remove and discard the seeds.  Slice into wedges, then cut off the rind with a sharp knife.

Arrange the melon wedges and radicchio leaves in 4 serving bowls, then arrange the crabmeat mixture on top.  Garnish with a few sprigs of fresh parsley and serve with crusty bread.

# prawn & rice salad

serves 4

**ingredients**

175 g/6 oz mixed long-grain and wild rice

salt and pepper

350 g/12 oz cooked, peeled prawns

1 mango, peeled, stoned and diced

4 spring onions, sliced

25 g/1 oz flaked almonds

1 tbsp finely chopped fresh mint

**for the dressing**

1 tbsp extra-virgin olive oil

2 tsp lime juice

1 garlic clove, crushed

1 tsp clear honey

salt and pepper

Cook the rice in a large saucepan of lightly salted boiling water for 35 minutes, or until tender. Drain and transfer to a large bowl, then add the prawns.

To make the dressing, mix all the ingredients together in a large jug, seasoning to taste with the salt and pepper, and whisk well until thoroughly blended. Pour the dressing over the rice and prawn mixture and leave to cool.

Add the mango, spring onions, almonds and mint to the salad and season to taste with pepper. Stir thoroughly, transfer to a large serving dish and serve.

# anchovy & olive salad

**serves 4**

**ingredients**

large handful of mixed lettuce leaves

12 cherry tomatoes, halved

20 black olives, stoned and halved

6 canned anchovy fillets, drained and
   thinly sliced

1 tbsp chopped fresh oregano

wedges of lemon, to garnish

crusty bread rolls, to serve

**for the dressing**

4 tbsp extra-virgin olive oil

1 tbsp white wine vinegar

1 tbsp lemon juice

1 tbsp chopped fresh flat-leaf parsley

salt and pepper

To make the dressing, put all the ingredients into a small bowl, season with salt and pepper and stir together well.

To assemble the salad, arrange the lettuce leaves in a serving dish. Scatter the cherry tomatoes on top, followed by the olives, anchovies and oregano. Drizzle over the dressing.

Transfer to individual plates, garnish with lemon wedges and serve with crusty bread rolls.

# smoked salmon &
# wild rocket salad

**serves 4**

**ingredients**

50 g/1¾ oz wild rocket leaves

1 tbsp chopped fresh flat-leaf parsley

2 spring onions, finely diced

2 large avocados

1 tbsp lemon juice

250 g/9 oz smoked salmon

**for the dressing**

150 ml/5 fl oz mayonnaise

2 tbsp lime juice

finely grated rind of 1 lime

1 tbsp chopped fresh flat-leaf parsley,
  plus extra sprigs to garnish

Shred the rocket and arrange in 4 individual glass bowls. Scatter over the chopped parsley and spring onions.

Halve, peel and stone the avocados and cut into thin slices or small chunks. Brush with the lemon juice to prevent discoloration, then divide between the salad bowls. Mix together gently. Cut the smoked salmon into strips and scatter over the top.

Put the mayonnaise in a bowl, then add the lime juice, lime rind and chopped parsley. Mix together well. Spoon some of the mayonnaise dressing on top of each salad and garnish with parsley sprigs.

# tuna & herbed fusilli salad

serves 4

**ingredients**

200 g/7 oz dried fusilli

1 red pepper, deseeded and quartered

1 red onion, sliced

4 tomatoes, sliced

200 g/7 oz canned tuna in brine,
    drained and flaked

**for the dressing**

6 tbsp basil-flavoured oil or
    extra-virgin olive oil

3 tbsp white wine vinegar

1 tbsp lime juice

1 tsp mustard

1 tsp honey

4 tbsp chopped fresh basil, plus extra
    sprigs to garnish

Bring a large saucepan of lightly salted water to the boil. Add the pasta, return to the boil and cook for 8–10 minutes until tender but still firm to the bite.

Meanwhile, put the pepper quarters under a preheated hot grill and cook for 10–12 minutes until the skins begin to blacken. Transfer to a polythene bag, seal and set aside.

Remove the pasta from the heat, drain and set aside to cool. Remove the pepper quarters from the bag and peel off the skins. Slice the pepper into strips.

To make the dressing, put all the dressing ingredients in a large bowl and stir together well. Add the pasta, pepper strips, onion, tomatoes and tuna. Toss together gently, then divide between serving bowls. Garnish with basil sprigs and serve.

# seafood & spinach salad

serves 4

**ingredients**

500 g/1 lb 2 oz live mussels, soaked
    and cleaned
100 g/3½ oz prawns, peeled and deveined
350 g/12 oz scallops
500 g/1 lb 2 oz baby spinach leaves
3 spring onions, trimmed and diced

**for the dressing**

4 tbsp extra-virgin olive oil
2 tbsp white wine vinegar
1 tbsp lemon juice
1 tsp finely grated lemon rind
1 garlic clove, chopped
1 tbsp grated fresh root ginger
1 small red chilli, deseeded and diced
1 tbsp chopped fresh coriander
salt and pepper

Put the mussels into a large pan with a little water, bring to the boil and cook over a high heat for 4 minutes. Drain and reserve the liquid. Discard any mussels that remain closed. Return the reserved liquid to the pan and bring to the boil. Add the prawns and scallops and cook for 3 minutes. Drain. Remove the mussels from their shells. Rinse the mussels, prawns and scallops in cold water, drain and put them in a large bowl. Cool, cover with clingfilm and chill for 45 minutes. Meanwhile, rinse the baby spinach leaves and transfer them to a pan with 4 tablespoons of water. Cook over a high heat for 1 minute, transfer to a colander, refresh under cold running water and drain.

To make the dressing, put all the ingredients into a small bowl and mix. Arrange the spinach on serving dishes, then scatter over half of the spring onions. Top with the mussels, prawns and scallops, then scatter over the remaining spring onions. Drizzle over the dressing and serve.

# neapolitan seafood salad

**serves 4**

**ingredients**

450 g/1 lb prepared squid, cut into strips

750 g/1 lb 10 oz cooked mussels

450 g/1 lb cooked cockles in brine

150 ml/5 fl oz white wine

300 ml/10 fl oz olive oil

225 g/8 oz dried campanelle or other
    small pasta shapes

juice of 1 lemon

1 bunch chives, snipped

1 bunch fresh parsley, finely chopped

salt and pepper

mixed salad leaves

4 large tomatoes, to garnish

Put all of the seafood into a large bowl, pour over the wine and half of the olive oil, and set aside for 6 hours.

Put the seafood mixture into a saucepan and simmer over a low heat for 10 minutes. Set aside to cool.

Bring a large saucepan of lightly salted water to the boil. Add the pasta and 1 tbsp of the remaining olive oil and cook for 8–10 minutes or until tender, but still firm to the bite. Drain thoroughly and refresh in cold water.

Strain off about half of the cooking liquid from the seafood and discard the rest. Mix in the lemon juice, chives, parsley and the remaining olive oil. Season to taste with salt and pepper. Drain the pasta and add to the seafood.

Cut the tomatoes into quarters. Shred the leaves and arrange them at the base of a salad bowl. Cut the tomatoes into quarters. Spoon the seafood salad into the bowl, garnish with the tomatoes and serve.

# mussel salad

serves 4

**ingredients**

2 large red peppers, deseeded and halved

350 g/12 oz cooked, shelled mussels,
    thawed if frozen

1 head radicchio

25 g/1 oz rocket

8 cooked green-lipped mussels in
    their shells

**for the dressing**

1 tbsp olive oil

1 tbsp lemon juice

1 tsp finely grated lemon rind

2 tsp clear honey

1 tsp French mustard

1 tbsp snipped fresh chives

salt and pepper

Put the peppers, skin-side up, on the grill rack and grill under a preheated hot grill for 8–10 minutes, or until the skin is charred and blistered and the flesh is soft. Remove from the rack with tongs, put into a bowl and cover with clingfilm. Leave for about 10 minutes, or until cool enough to handle, then peel off the skins.

Slice the pepper flesh into thin strips and put into a bowl. Gently stir in the shelled mussels.

To make the dressing, whisk the oil, lemon juice and rind, honey, mustard and chives together in a bowl until well blended. Season to taste with salt and pepper. Add the pepper and mussel mixture and toss gently until well coated.

Remove the central core of the radicchio and shred the leaves. Put into a serving bowl with the rocket and toss together.

Pile the mussel mixture into the centre of the leaves and arrange the green-lipped mussels in their shells around the edge of the bowl.

# sweet & sour fish salad

**serves 4**

**ingredients**

225 g/8 oz trout fillets

225 g/8 oz white fish fillets
  (such as haddock or cod)

300 ml/½ pint water

1 stalk lemon grass

2 lime leaves

1 large red chilli

1 bunch spring onions, trimmed
  and shredded

115 g/4 oz fresh pineapple flesh, diced

1 small red pepper, deseeded and diced

1 bunch watercress, washed and trimmed

fresh snipped chives, to garnish

**for the dressing**

1 tbsp sunflower oil

1 tbsp rice wine vinegar

pinch of chilli powder

1 tsp clear honey

salt and pepper

Rinse the fish, place in a frying pan and pour over the water. Bend the lemon grass in half to bruise it and add to the pan with the lime leaves. Prick the chilli with a fork and add to the pan. Bring to the boil and simmer for 7–8 minutes. Let cool.

Drain the fish fillet thoroughly, flake the flesh away from the skin and place in a bowl. Gently stir in the spring onions, pineapple and pepper.

Arrange the washed watercress on 4 serving plates and spoon the cooked fish mixture on top.

To make the dressing, mix all the ingredients together, seasoning well. Spoon over the fish and serve garnished with chives.

# chilli prawns with pineapple & papaya salsa

**serves 8**

**ingredients**

4 tbsp sunflower oil

1 fresh red chilli, deseeded and chopped

1 garlic clove, crushed

48 prawns

chopped fresh parsley, to garnish

**for the pineapple & papaya salsa**

1 large papaya, halved, deseeded, peeled
    and cut into 5 mm/¼ inch dice

1 small pineapple, halved, cored, peeled
    and cut into 5 mm/¼ inch dice

2 spring onions, very finely chopped

1 red chilli, or to taste, deseeded and
    finely chopped

1 garlic clove, very finely chopped

2½ tsp lemon juice

½ tsp ground cumin

¼ tsp salt

black pepper

To make the salsa, put the papaya in a large bowl with the pineapple, spring onions, chilli, garlic, lemon juice, cumin, salt and pepper. Adjust the lemon juice, cumin, salt or pepper to taste, if necessary. Cover and chill until required, ideally at least 2 hours.

Heat a wok over a high heat. Add the oil and swirl around, then add the chilli and garlic and stir-fry for 20 seconds. Add the prawns and stir-fry for 2–3 minutes until the prawns are cooked through, become pink and curl.

Tip the prawns, garlic and any oil left in the wok into a heatproof bowl and leave the prawns to cool and marinate in the chilli oil. When the prawns are completely cool, cover the bowl and chill for at least 2 hours.

When ready to serve, give the salsa a stir and adjust the seasoning, if necessary. Arrange a mound of salsa on each of 8 plates. Remove the prawns from the marinade and divide between plates. Sprinkle with parsley and serve.

# seared swordfish with fresh tomato salsa

serves 4

**ingredients**
4 boneless swordfish steaks,
    about 140 g/5 oz each
salt and pepper
knob of butter
1 tbsp olive oil
slices of crusty bread, to serve

**for the fresh tomato & olive salsa**
4 tbsp extra-virgin olive oil
1 tbsp red-wine vinegar
600 g/1 lb 5 oz ripe, juicy beef tomatoes,
    cored, deseeded and finely chopped
140 g/5 oz large black olives, stoned and
    cut in half
1 shallot, finely chopped or thinly sliced
1 tbsp capers in brine, rinsed and dried
salt and pepper
3 tbsp finely shredded fresh basil leaves

To make the fresh tomato & olive salsa, whisk the olive oil and vinegar together in a bowl large enough to hold all the ingredients. Gently stir in the tomatoes, olives, shallot and capers with salt and pepper to taste. Cover and chill until required.

Season the swordfish steaks on both sides with salt. Melt the butter with the oil in frying pan large enough to hold the swordfish steaks in a single layer. (If you don't have a large enough pan, cook the steaks in 2 batches.)

Add the swordfish steaks to the pan in a single layer and fry for 5 minutes, or until golden brown, then carefully turn the fish over and continue frying about 3 minutes longer until the fish is cooked through and flakes easily. Remove the fish from the pan and set aside to cool completely. Cover and chill for at least 2 hours.

When ready to serve, remove the fish from the fridge at least 15 minutes in advance. Stir the basil into the salsa, then adjust the seasoning if necessary. Break the swordfish into large flakes and gently stir into the salsa – take care not to break up the fish too much. Arrange the fish salad in 4 bowls, spooning over any of the leftover juices and serve with slices of crusty bread.

# prawn cocktail salad

**serves 4**

**ingredients**

2 tsp salt

½ lemon, sliced

32 large shelled and deveined prawns,
    thawed if frozen

175 g/6 oz tomato ketchup

1½ tbsp grated horseradish

3 celery sticks, cut into 5 mm/
    ¼ inch slices

finely grated rind and juice of 1 lemon

salt and pepper

iceberg lettuce leaves, shredded, to serve

lemon wedges, to garnish

Bring a large pan of water to a rolling boil. Stir in the salt and lemon slices, then reduce the heat to low. Add the prawns and leave to simmer for about 3 minutes until they are cooked through, turn pink and curl. Drain the prawns into a large colander and immediately refresh under cold running water to stop the cooking and cool the prawns; set aside.

Put the ketchup, horseradish, celery and lemon rind in a bowl and stir together. Stir in 1 tablespoon lemon juice, then add more juice and salt and pepper to taste. Stir in the prawns, then cover and chill for at least 2 hours.

When ready to serve, stir the prawn salad and adjust the seasoning, if necessary. Divide the shredded lettuce between 4 glass bowls and spoon the salad on top. Serve at once while the salad is still chilled, with lemon wedges for squeezing over.

# celeriac rémoulade with crab

**serves 4**

**ingredients**

450 g/1 lb celeric, peeled and grated
juice of 1 lemon
250 g/9 oz fresh white crabmeat,
   picked over
chopped fresh dill or parsley, to garnish

**for the rémoulade dressing**

150 ml/5 fl oz mayonnaise
1 tbsp Dijon mustard
1½ tsp white wine vinegar
2 tbsp capers in brine, well rinsed
salt and white pepper

To make the dressing, put the mayonnaise in a bowl. Beat in the mustard, vinegar and capers with salt and white pepper to taste – the mixture should be piquant with a strong mustard flavour. Cover and chill until required.

Bring a large pan of salted water to a full, rolling boil. Meanwhile, peel the celeriac and cut it into quarters, then grate it either in a food processor or on the coarse side of a box grater.

Add the grated celeriac and lemon juice to the water and blanch for 1½–2 minutes until it is just slightly tender. Rinse the celeriac well, then put it under cold running water to stop the cooking. Use your hands to squeeze out the excess moisture, then pat the celeriac dry with kitchen paper or a clean tea towel.

Stir the celeriac into the dressing, along with the crabmeat. Taste and adjust the seasoning, if necessary. Cover and chill for at least 30 minutes.

When ready to serve, spoon into bowls and sprinkle with dill or parsley.

# health-
# boosting
a collection of energizing salads

# wild rice salad with cucumber & orange

**serves 4**

**ingredients**

225 g/8 oz wild rice

850 ml/1½ pints water

1 each red, yellow and orange peppers,
   skinned, deseeded and thinly sliced

½ cucumber, halved lengthways and sliced

1 orange, peeled, pith removed and cubed

3 ripe tomatoes, cut into chunks

1 red onion, chopped very finely

generous handful of chopped
   flat-leaf parsley

**for the dressing**

1 clove garlic, crushed

1 tbsp balsamic vinegar

sea salt and black pepper

2 tbsp extra-virgin olive oil

salt and pepper

Put the wild rice and water into a large pan and bring to the boil. Stir, cover and simmer for about 40 minutes or until the rice is al dente (firm to the bite). Uncover the rice for the last few minutes of cooking to allow any excess water to evaporate.

To make the dressing, put the crushed garlic, vinegar, olive oil and seasoning into a screwtop jar and shake vigorously. Add extra vinegar, oil or seasoning as required.

Drain the rice and turn into a large bowl. Pour over the dressing and mix in. Then mix in the chopped peppers, cucumber, orange, tomatoes, red onion and flat-leaf parsley and serve.

# red pepper & radicchio salad

**serves 4**

**ingredients**

2 red peppers

1 head radicchio, separated into leaves

4 cooked whole beetroot,
   cut into matchsticks

12 radishes, sliced

4 spring onions, finely chopped

4 tbsp basic salad dressing

crusty bread, to serve

Core and deseed the peppers and cut into rounds.

Arrange the radicchio leaves in a salad bowl. Add the pepper, beetroot, radishes and spring onions. Drizzle with the dressing and serve with crusty bread.

# spring clean salad

**serves 4**

**ingredients**

2 dessert apples, cored and diced

juice of 1 lemon

large chunk of watermelon,
    deseeded and cubed

1 head chicory, sliced into rounds

4 sticks celery with leaves,
    roughly chopped

1 tbsp walnut oil

Core and dice the apples, place in a bowl and pour over the lemon juice. Mix well to prevent discoloration.

Add the rest of the fruit and vegetables to the bowl and mix gently. Pour in the walnut oil, mix again and serve.

# chickpea & tomato salad

**serves 4**

**ingredients**

175 g/6 oz dried chickpeas or
    400 g/14 oz canned, drained and rinsed
225 g/8 oz ripe tomatoes,
    roughly chopped
1 red onion, thinly sliced
handful of fresh basil leaves, torn
1 cos or romaine lettuce, torn
crusty bread, to serve

**for the dressing**

1 green chilli, deseeded and
    finely chopped
1 clove garlic, crushed
juice and zest of 2 lemons
2 tbsp olive oil
1 tbsp water
black pepper

If using dried chickpeas, soak overnight then boil for at least 30 minutes until soft. Leave to cool.

Put the chilli, garlic, lemon juice, olive oil, water and black pepper in a screwtop jar and shake vigorously. Taste and add more lemon juice or oil if necessary.

Add the tomatoes, onion and basil to the chickpeas and mix gently. Pour over the dressing and mix again. Arrange on a bed of lettuce and serve with crusty bread.

# fennel & orange salad

serves 4

**ingredients**

2 oranges, peeled and sliced

1 bulb Florence fennel, thinly sliced

1 red onion, peeled and sliced
   into thin rings

**for the dressing**

juice of 1 orange

2 tbsp balsamic vinegar

Arrange the orange slices in the bottom of a shallow dish. Place a layer of fennel on top and then add a layer of onion.

Mix the orange juice with the vinegar and drizzle over the salad.

# warm new potato & lentil salad

**serves 4**

**ingredients**
85 g/3 oz puy lentils
450 g/1 lb new potatoes
6 spring onions
1 tbsp olive oil
2 tbsp balsamic vinegar
salt and pepper

Bring a large pan of water to the boil. Rinse the lentils then cook for about 20 minutes or until tender. Drain, rinse and leave to one side.

Meanwhile, steam or boil the potatoes until they are soft right through. Drain and halve.

Trim the base from the spring onions and cut in long strips.

Put the lentils, potatoes and spring onions into a serving dish and toss with the olive oil and vinegar. Season with plenty of black pepper and a little salt if required.

# beansprout, apricot & almond salad

serves 4

**ingredients**

115 g/4 oz beansprouts, washed and dried

small bunch seedless black and
    green grapes, halved

12 unsulphured dried apricots, halved

25 g/1 oz blanched almonds, halved

black pepper

**for the dressing**

1 tbsp walnut oil

1 tsp sesame oil

2 tsp balsamic vinegar

Place the beansprouts in the bottom of a large salad bowl and sprinkle the grapes and apricots on top.

Place the oils and vinegar in a screwtop jar and shake vigorously to mix. Pour over the salad.

Scatter over the almonds and season with freshly ground black pepper.

# asparagus & tomato salad

**ingredients**

225 g/8 oz asparagus spears

1 lamb's lettuce, washed and torn

25 g/1 oz rocket or mizuna leaves

450 g/1 lb ripe tomatoes, sliced

12 black olives, stoned and chopped

1 tbsp toasted pine kernels

**for the dressing**

1 tsp lemon oil

1 tbsp olive oil

1 tsp wholegrain mustard

2 tbsp balsamic vinegar

salt and pepper

Steam the asparagus spears for about 8 minutes or until tender. Rinse under cold running water to prevent them cooking any further, then cut into 5-cm/2-inch pieces.

Arrange the lettuce and rocket leaves around a salad platter to form the base of the salad. Place the sliced tomatoes in a circle on top and the asparagus in the centre.

Sprinkle the black olives and pine kernels over the top. Put the lemon oil, olive oil, mustard and vinegar in a screwtop jar and season to taste with sea salt and black pepper. Shake vigorously and drizzle over the salad.

# avocado salad

**ingredients**

large handful of radicchio leaves

large handful of rocket leaves

1 small galia melon

2 ripe avocados

1 tbsp lemon juice

200 g/7 oz fontina cheese,
    cut into bite-sized pieces

**for the dressing**

5 tbsp lemon-flavoured or
    extra-virgin olive oil

1 tbsp white wine vinegar

1 tbsp lemon juice

1 tbsp chopped fresh parsley

To make the dressing, mix together the oil, vinegar, lemon juice and parsley in a small bowl.

Arrange the radicchio and rocket on serving plates. Halve and deseed the melon, then cut the flesh from the skin. Discard the skin. Slice the melon flesh and arrange it over the salad leaves.

Cut the avocados in half and remove and discard the stones and skin. Slice the flesh and brush with lemon juice. Arrange the slices over the melon, then scatter over the cheese. Drizzle over the dressing, garnish with chopped fresh parsley and serve.

# herby potato salad

**ingredients**

500 g/1 lb 2 oz new potatoes

salt and pepper

16 vine-ripened cherry tomatoes, halved

70 g/2½ oz black olives, stoned and
    coarsely chopped

4 spring onions, finely sliced

2 tbsp chopped fresh mint

2 tbsp chopped fresh parsley

2 tbsp chopped fresh coriander

juice of 1 lemon

3 tbsp extra-virgin olive oil

Cook the potatoes in a saucepan of lightly salted boiling water for 15 minutes, or until tender. Drain, then leave to cool slightly before peeling off the skins. Cut into halves or quarters, depending on the size of the potato. Then combine with the tomatoes, olives, spring onions and herbs in a salad bowl.

Mix the lemon juice and oil together in a small bowl or jug and pour over the potato salad. Season to taste with salt and pepper before serving.

# tabbouleh

**ingredients**

175 g/6 oz quinoa

600 ml/1 pint water

10 vine-ripened cherry tomatoes, deseeded
   and halved

7.5-cm/3-inch piece cucumber, diced

3 spring onions, finely chopped

juice of ½ lemon

2 tbsp extra-virgin olive oil

4 tbsp chopped fresh mint

4 tbsp chopped fresh coriander

4 tbsp chopped fresh parsley

salt and pepper

Put the quinoa into a medium-sized saucepan and cover with the water. Bring to the boil, then reduce the heat, cover and simmer over a low heat for 15 minutes. Drain if necessary.

Leave the quinoa to cool slightly before combining with the remaining ingredients in a salad bowl. Adjust the seasoning, if necessary, before serving.

# buckwheat noodle salad with smoked tofu

**serves 2**

**ingredients**

200 g/7 oz buckwheat noodles

250 g/9 oz firm smoked tofu
   (drained weight)

200 g/7 oz white cabbage, finely shredded

250 g/9 oz carrots, finely shredded

3 spring onions, diagonally sliced

1 fresh red chilli, deseeded and
   finely sliced into rounds

2 tbsp sesame seeds, lightly toasted

**for the dressing**

1 tsp grated fresh root ginger

1 garlic clove, crushed

175 g/6 oz silken tofu (drained weight)

4 tsp tamari (wheat-free soy sauce)

2 tbsp sesame oil

4 tbsp hot water

salt

Cook the noodles in a large saucepan of lightly salted boiling water according to the packet instructions. Drain and refresh under cold running water.

To make the dressing, blend the ginger, garlic, silken tofu, soy sauce, oil and water together in a small bowl until smooth and creamy. Season to taste with salt.

Place the smoked tofu in a steamer. Steam for 5 minutes, then cut into thin slices.

Meanwhile, put the cabbage, carrots, spring onions and chilli into a bowl and toss to mix. To serve, arrange the noodles on serving plates and top with the carrot salad and slices of tofu. Spoon over the dressing and sprinkle with sesame seeds.

# courgette & mint salad

serves 4

**ingredients**

2 courgettes, cut into batons

100 g/3½ oz green beans, cut into thirds

1 green pepper, deseeded and
    cut into strips

2 celery sticks, sliced

1 bunch of watercress

**for the dressing**

200 ml/7 fl oz natural yogurt

1 garlic clove, crushed

2 tbsp chopped fresh mint

pepper

Cook the courgette batons and beans in a saucepan of lightly salted water for 7–8 minutes. Drain, rinse under cold running water and drain again. Leave to cool completely.

Mix the courgettes and beans with the green pepper strips, celery and watercress in a large serving bowl.

To make the dressing, combine the yogurt, garlic and mint in a small bowl. Season to taste with pepper.

Spoon the dressing onto the salad and serve immediately.

# tomato, mozzarella & avocado salad

serves 4

ingredients

2 ripe beef tomatoes

100 g/3½ oz mozzarella cheese

2 avocados

few fresh basil leaves, torn into pieces

20 black olives

fresh crusty bread, to serve

for the dressing

1 tbsp olive oil

1½ tbsp white wine vinegar

1 tsp coarse grain mustard

salt and pepper

Using a sharp knife, cut the tomatoes into thick wedges and place in a large serving dish. Drain the mozzarella cheese and roughly tear into pieces. Cut the avocados in half and remove the stones. Cut the flesh into slices, then arrange the mozzarella cheese and avocado with the tomatoes.

Mix the oil, vinegar and mustard together in a small bowl, add salt and pepper to taste, then drizzle over the salad.

Scatter the basil and olives over the top and serve immediately with fresh crusty bread.

# roasted vegetable salad

**serves 4**

**ingredients**

1 onion

1 aubergine, about 225 g/8 oz

1 red pepper, deseeded

1 orange pepper, deseeded

1 large courgette, about 175 g/6 oz

2–4 garlic cloves

2–4 tbsp olive oil

salt and pepper

1 tbsp shredded fresh basil

freshly shaved Parmesan cheese, to serve

fresh crusty bread, to serve

**for the dressing**

1 tbsp balsamic vinegar

2 tbsp extra-virgin olive oil

salt and pepper

Preheat the oven to 200°C/400°F/Gas Mark 6. Cut all the vegetables into even-sized wedges, put into a roasting tin and scatter over the garlic.

Pour over 2 tablespoons of the olive oil and turn the vegetables in the oil until well coated. Add a little salt and pepper. Roast in the preheated oven for 40 minutes, or until tender, adding the extra olive oil if becoming too dry.

Meanwhile, put the vinegar, extra virgin olive oil and salt and pepper to taste into a screw-top jar and shake until blended.

Once the vegetables are cooked, remove from the oven, arrange on a serving dish and pour over the dressing. Sprinkle with the basil and serve with shavings of Parmesan cheese. Serve warm or cold with fresh crusty bread.

# three bean salad

serves 4 - 6

**ingredients**

175 g/6 oz mixed salad leaves, such as
    spinach, rocket and frisée

1 red onion

85 g/3 oz radishes

175 g/6 oz cherry tomatoes

115 g/4 oz cooked beetroot

280 g/10 oz canned cannellini beans,
    drained and rinsed

200 g/7 oz canned red kidney beans,
    drained and rinsed

300 g/10$\frac{1}{2}$ oz canned flageolet beans,
    drained and rinsed

40 g/1$\frac{1}{2}$ oz dried cranberries

55 g/2 oz roasted cashew nuts

225 g/8 oz feta cheese (drained weight),
    crumbled

**for the dressing**

4 tbsp extra-virgin olive oil

1 tsp Dijon mustard

2 tbsp lemon juice

1 tbsp chopped fresh coriander

salt and pepper

Arrange the salad leaves in a salad bowl and reserve.

Thinly slice the onion, then cut in half to form half moons and put into a bowl.

Thinly slice the radishes, cut the tomatoes in half and peel the beetroot, if necessary, and dice. Add to the onion with the remaining ingredients, except the nuts and cheese.

Put all the ingredients for the dressing into a screw-top jar and shake until blended. Pour over the bean mixture, toss lightly, then spoon on top of the salad leaves.

Scatter over the nuts and cheese and serve immediately.

# succatash salad

**ingredients**

1 tbsp cider vinegar

1 tsp wholegrain mustard

1 tsp sugar

3 tbsp garlic-flavoured olive oil

1 tbsp sunflower oil

400 g/14 oz canned sweetcorn kernels,
    rinsed and drained

400 g/14 oz runner beans, finely chopped

2 peeled red peppers from a jar, drained
    and finely chopped

2 spring onions, very finely chopped

salt and pepper

2 tbsp chopped fresh parsley, to garnish

Beat the vinegar, mustard and sugar together. Gradually whisk in the olive and sunflower oils to form an emulsion.

Stir in the sweetcorn kernels, runner beans, red peppers and spring onions. Add salt and pepper to taste and stir together again. Cover and chill for up to one day until required.

When ready to serve, adjust the seasoning, if necessary, and stir in the parsley.

# spinach salad with blue cheese dressing

**serves 4 – 6**

**ingredients**

300 g/10 oz bag baby spinach leaves,
   any thick stems or yellow leaves
   removed, then well rinsed and dried
4 spring onions, chopped
3 oranges, segmented
55 g/2 oz sunflower seeds

**for the blue cheese dressing**

125 g/4½ oz full-flavoured blue cheese,
   such as Roquefort, crumbled
200 g/7 oz Greek yogurt
1 tbsp white wine vinegar
½ onion, grated
½ small bunch fresh chives, chopped
salt and pepper

To make the dressing, put the blue cheese, yogurt, vinegar and onion in a blender or food processor and blend until smooth. Add the chives and give another quick blitz. Season with salt and pepper to taste. Cover and chill until required.

When you are ready to assemble the salad, place the spinach leaves and spring onions in a salad bowl and toss with half the dressing. Transfer to a serving bowl and top with the orange segments and a sprinkling of sunflower seeds.

Pass the remaining dressing separately for spooning over individual portions, if desired.

# pear & roquefort salad

**serves 4**

**ingredients**
few leaves of lollo rosso
few leaves of radicchio
few leaves of lamb's lettuce
2 ripe pears
pepper
whole fresh chives, to garnish

**for the dressing**
55 g/2 oz Roquefort cheese
150 ml/5 fl oz natural yogurt
2 tbsp snipped fresh chives
pepper

Place the cheese in a bowl and mash with a fork. Gradually blend the yogurt into the cheese to make a smooth dressing. Add the chives and season with pepper to taste.

Tear the lollo rosso, radicchio and lamb's lettuce leaves into manageable pieces. Arrange the salad leaves on a large serving platter or divide them between individual serving plates.

Cut the pears into quarters and remove the cores. Cut the quarters into slices. Arrange the pear slices over the salad leaves.

Drizzle the Roquefort dressing over the pears and garnish with a few whole chives.

# green fruit salad

**serves 4**

**ingredients**
1 honeydew melon
2 green apples
2 kiwi fruit
125 g/4½ oz seedless white grapes
fresh mint sprigs, to decorate

**for the syrup dressing**
1 lemon
150 ml/5 fl oz white wine
150 ml/5 fl oz water
4 tbsp clear honey
few sprigs of fresh mint

To make the syrup, pare the rind from the lemon using a potato peeler.

Put the lemon rind in a saucepan with the white wine, water and clear honey. Bring to the boil, then simmer gently for 10 minutes.

Remove the syrup from the heat. Add the sprigs of mint and leave to cool.

To prepare the fruit, first cut the melon in half and scoop out the seeds. Use a melon baller or a teaspoon to make melon balls.

Core and chop the apples. Peel and slice the kiwi fruit.

Strain the cooled syrup into a serving bowl, removing and reserving the lemon rind and discarding the mint sprigs.

Add the apple, grapes, kiwi fruit and melon to the serving bowl. Stir through gently to mix.

Serve the fruit salad, decorated with sprigs of fresh mint and some of the reserved lemon rind.

# tropical fruit salad

**serves 4**

**ingredients**

1 papaya

1 mango

1 pineapple

4 oranges, peeled and cut into segments

125 g/4½ oz strawberries, hulled
  and quartered

single or double cream, to serve (optional)

**for the syrup dressing**

6 tbsp caster sugar

400 ml/14 fl oz water

½ tsp ground mixed spice

grated rind of ½ lemon

Put the sugar, water, mixed spice and lemon rind into a saucepan. Bring to the boil, stirring continuously, then continue to boil for 1 minute. Remove from the heat and leave to cool to room temperature. Transfer to a jug or bowl, cover with clingfilm and chill in the refrigerator for at least 1 hour.

Peel and halve the papaya and remove the seeds. Cut the flesh into small chunks or slices, and put into a large bowl. Cut the mango twice lengthways, close to the stone. Remove and discard the stone. Peel and cut the flesh into small chunks or slices, and add to the bowl. Cut off the top and bottom of the pineapple and remove the hard skin. Cut the pineapple in half lengthways, then into quarters, and remove the tough core. Cut the remaining flesh into small pieces and add to the bowl. Add the orange segments and strawberries.

Pour over the chilled syrup, cover with clingfilm and chill until required. Serve with single or double cream, if using.

# fig & watermelon salad

**serves 4**

**ingredients**
1 watermelon, weighing about
    1.5 kg/3 lb 5 oz
115 g/4 oz seedless black grapes
4 figs

**for the syrup dressing**
1 lime
grated rind and juice of 1 orange
1 tbsp maple syrup
2 tbsp clear honey

Cut the watermelon into quarters and scoop out and discard the seeds. Cut the flesh away from the rind, then chop the flesh into 2.5-cm/1-inch cubes. Place the watermelon cubes in a bowl with the grapes. Cut each fig lengthways into 8 wedges and add to the bowl.

Grate the lime rind and mix it with the orange rind and juice, maple syrup and honey in a small saucepan. Bring to the boil over a low heat. Pour the mixture over the fruit and stir. Leave to cool. Stir again, cover and chill in the refrigerator for at least 1 hour, stirring occasionally.

Divide the fruit salad equally between 4 bowls, and serve.

# melon & mango salad

serves 4

**ingredients**

1 cantaloupe melon
55 g/2 oz black grapes, halved and seeded
55 g/2 oz green grapes
1 large mango
1 bunch watercress, trimmed
iceberg lettuce leaves, shredded
1 passion fruit

**for the melon dressing**

150 ml/5 fl oz natural yogurt
1 tbsp clear honey
1 tsp grated fresh root ginger

**for the salad leaves dressing**

2 tbsp olive oil
1 tbsp cider vinegar
salt and pepper

To make the dressing for the melon, whisk together the yogurt, honey and ginger in a small bowl.

Halve the melon, scoop out the seeds with a spoon and discard. Slice, peel and dice the flesh. Place in a bowl with the grapes.

Slice the mango on each side of its large flat stone. On each mango half, slash the flesh into a criss-cross pattern, down to but not through the skin. Push the skin from underneath to turn the mango halves inside out. Now remove the flesh and add to the melon mixture.

Arrange the watercress and lettuce leaves on 4 serving plates.

Make the dressing for the salad leaves by whisking together the olive oil and vinegar with a little salt and pepper. Drizzle over the salad leaves.

Divide the melon mixture between the 4 plates and spoon over the yogurt dressing.

Scoop the seeds out of the passion fruit and sprinkle them over the salads. Serve immediately or chill in the refrigerator until required.

# papaya salad

serves 4

**ingredients**

1 crisp lettuce

¼ small white cabbage

2 papayas

2 tomatoes

25 g/1 oz roasted peanuts, chopped
    roughly

4 spring onions, trimmed and sliced thinly

basil leaves, to garnish

**for the dressing**

4 tbsp olive oil

1 tbsp fish sauce or light soy sauce

2 tbsp lime or lemon juice

1 tbsp dark muscovado sugar

1 tsp finely chopped fresh red or
    green chilli

To make the dressing, whisk together the oil, fish sauce or soy sauce, lime or lemon juice, sugar and chilli. Set aside, stirring occasionally to dissolve the sugar.

Shred the lettuce and white cabbage, then toss together and arrange on a large serving plate.

Peel the papayas and slice them in half. Scoop out the seeds, then slice the flesh thinly. Arrange on top of the lettuce and cabbage.

Soak the tomatoes in a bowl of boiling water for 1 minute, then lift out and peel. Remove the seeds and chop the flesh. Arrange on the salad leaves.

Scatter the peanuts and spring onions over the top. Whisk the dressing and pour over the salad. Garnish with basil leaves and serve at once.

# exotic fruit cocktail

**serves 4**

**ingredients**

2 oranges

2 large passion fruit

1 pineapple

1 pomegranate

1 banana

Cut 1 orange in half and squeeze the juice into a bowl, discarding any pips. Using a sharp knife, cut away all the peel and pith from the second orange. Working over the bowl to catch the juice, carefully cut the orange segments between the membranes to obtain skinless segments of fruit. Discard any pips.

Cut the passion fruit in half, scoop the flesh into a nylon sieve and, using a spoon, push the pulp and juice into the bowl of orange segments. Discard the pips.

Using a sharp knife, cut away all the skin from the pineapple and cut the flesh lengthways into quarters. Cut away the central hard core. Cut the flesh into chunks and add to the orange and passion fruit mixture. Cover and refrigerate the fruit at this stage if you are not serving immediately.

Cut the pomegranate into quarters and, using your fingers or a teaspoon, remove the red seeds from the membrane. Cover and refrigerate until ready to serve – do not add too early to the fruit cocktail as the seeds discolour the other fruit.

Just before serving, peel and slice the banana, add to the fruit cocktail with the pomegranate seeds and mix thoroughly. Serve immediately.

# melon & strawberry salad

**serves 4**

**ingredients**
½ iceberg lettuce, shredded
1 small honeydew melon
225 g/8 oz strawberries, sliced
5 cm/2 inch piece cucumber,
    thinly sliced
fresh mint sprigs, to garnish

**for the dressing**
200 g/7 fl oz natural yogurt
5 cm/2 inch piece cucumber, peeled
a few fresh mint leaves
½ tsp finely grated lime or lemon rind
pinch of caster sugar
3–4 ice cubes

Arrange the shredded lettuce on 4 serving plates.

Cut the melon lengthways into quarters. Scoop out the seeds and cut through the flesh down to the skin at 2.5-cm/1-inch intervals. Cut the melon close to the skin and detach the flesh.

Place the chunks of melon on the beds of lettuce with the strawberries and cucumber slices.

To make the dressing, put the yogurt, cucumber, mint leaves, lime or lemon rind, caster sugar and ice cubes into a blender or food processor. Blend together for about 15 seconds until smooth. Alternatively, chop the cucumber and mint finely, crush the ice cubes and combine with the other ingredients.

Serve the salad with a little dressing poured over it. Garnish with sprigs of fresh mint.

# index